PENGUIN REFERENCE BOOKS
Plain English: A User's Guide

Philip Davies Roberts grew up in Quebec near the New England border and spent his formative years in Nova Scotia. He was educated at Acadia University in that province and at Jesus College, Oxford. He has worked in Spain as an English teacher; in England as a school-teacher, a journalist (with Reuters) and a public relations executive; in Australia as a university lecturer specializing in English language and poetics; and in Costa Rica as a reporter for the *Tico Times*. He now lives in Annapolis Royal, Nova Scotia, where he works as a freelance writer, music teacher, organist and choir director. In 1986 he received a Canada Council grant to write and produce for a season a bilingual stage adaptation of North America's first drama, *Le Théâtre de Neptune en la Nouvelle France* by Marc Lescarbot. (The play, a masque, was first performed on the waters of Port Royal – now the Annapolis River Basin – in 1606.) His book *How Poetry Works* is published in Pelican and an annotated edition of traditional nursery songs with music is planned for publication by Penguin. His poetry has been widely published in Britain, Australia, the USA and Canada.

Philip Davies Roberts

Plain English:
a User's Guide

Penguin Books

Penguin Books Ltd, Harmondsworth, Middlesex, England
Viking Penguin Inc., 40 West 23rd Street, New York, New York 10010, U.S.A.
Penguin Books Australia Ltd, Ringwood, Victoria, Australia
Penguin Books Canada Limited, 2801 John Street, Markham, Ontario, Canada L3R 1B4
Penguin Books (N.Z.) Ltd, 182–190 Wairau Road, Auckland 10, New Zealand

First published 1987

Typeset, printed and bound in Great Britain by
Hazell Watson & Viney Ltd,
Member of BPCC Group
Aylesbury, Bucks
Filmset in Linotron 202 Baskerville

Contents

To T. C. Perkins – outstanding teacher and friend

Acknowledgements

My thanks go to Jüri Gabriel in Britain, Helen Amoriggi, Joel Bonn, and Charlotte and David Haley in Canada, Stephen Knight in Australia, and Gene McDaniel in the USA, for their generous help. My thanks too to Thomas Barr III.

Foreword

English is spoken in countless dialects all over the world. Each dialect contributes to a specific national culture. Working together, they give life to the global tongue we call English. This is the English that unites us and makes us a family.

The two super-dialects of English today are American (principally the dialects of Canada and the USA) and British (those of the rest of the English-speaking world). Each of these is made up of many dialects and sub-dialects. There are striking differences between English dialects, but, in spite of this, all of them adhere to certain standard principles. This book is based on those principles.

I've arranged my material so that you may find help for a specific problem quickly. The first section, GRAMMAR, covers the standard terminology we use to discuss how English works. The next, VOCABULARY, is a midget dictionary of words which seem to cause the most trouble. This is the largest section of the book, and will probably turn out to be the most useful to the average user in the long run. TYPOGRAPHY, which follows, is a guide to how such things as capitals, colons, commas, and italics are used in written and printed English. (I've heard it said that anyone who takes the comma seriously must be insane. Possibly, but wrongly placed commas, or a lack of them, can completely alter the meaning of a sentence.) DIALECTS is a brief account of the main distinguishing features of American and British, including the dialects of Australia, Canada, Eire, New Zealand, South Africa, the United Kingdom, and the United States. STYLE, the final section in the main part of the book, offers a few suggestions for improving your writing ability.

At the back of the book you will find help with more specific matters, particularly writing letters, reports, and essays. There is also a list of other useful books, as well as a glossary of the main grammatical terms used in the rest of the book. Then comes the index. When in doubt about something, look there: it'll tell you where to go for help. Finally, on the inside back cover is a list of the principal parts of the main irregular verbs in English.

In a book as short as this it's impossible to include everything. I say very little about spelling and nothing at all about pronunciation: this is where your dictionary comes in. It goes without saying that you must have a good English dictionary, and that you must get used to consulting it frequently. Everyone has to, even the experts. For British English get the most recent edition of *The Concise Oxford Dictionary*, published by Oxford University Press. For American English get *Webster's New Collegiate Dictionary*, published by Merriam-Webster. The true devotee of English will have both within easy reach. You'll also find many interesting and lively books on British and American English, as well as books about Australian, Canadian, South African, and other national dialects; some of these are listed on pages 181–5.

The importance of acquiring a working knowledge of standard English has been well expressed by Robert Clairborne in his very readable book *Our Marvelous Native Tongue: The Life and Times of the English Language:*

Though most English speakers *speak* some nonstandard dialect, they almost certainly *understand* the educated speech of their region and, if they're literate, written Standard English. (The latter, in fact, is acceptable currency almost anywhere in the English-speaking world.) The overwhelming majority of English-language publications—newspapers, magazines, and books—are written, apart from some dialogue passages, in Standard English. . . . Students unquestionably have a right to use their own "language" (i.e., dialect), and in fact most of them continue to use it at home and around the neighborhood. But they also have an equal right to learn to read and write the only "language" that can serve them beyond the boundaries of their own neighborhood or occupational or ethnic group.

A note of caution: even the most highly regarded experts frequently depart from the supposed canons of standard English, particularly in informal conversation. It's generally considered impolite to "correct" or otherwise draw attention to other people's English usage where it differs from your own. The implication is that you view your own English as somehow superior to the other person's, which may reveal more of your attitude to others than you would like. So, please, use your linguistic capabilities with discretion, wisdom, and kindness. Concentrate on communicating your own meaning as clearly, directly, and simply as possible.

Grammar

Grammar is an attempt to understand how language functions. There are two approaches to it, the **descriptive** and the **prescriptive**. A descriptive grammar of a language tries to understand how people actually speak and write. In other words, it observes how language is used in everyday situations, and then uses these factual observations to build an all-inclusive set of principles capable of explaining how a language works and how we acquire this information.

A prescriptive approach, on the other hand, tries to work out definitive principles for an "accepted" or "standard" form of a language, usually based on the way educated people speak and write. These principles will reflect how much these educated people are aware of the history and traditions of that language, and how ready they are to accept changing standards. The fact that a large part of the general population may be quite ignorant of the views of these educated people doesn't really matter: prescriptive grammar mainly serves to isolate a generalized English which may be seen as underlying all the actual dialects of which the language is composed, dialects which may be incomprehensible to people in other parts of the English-speaking world.

The advantage of a prescriptive grammar of English is that it can quickly communicate the essentials of what is standard, or universally acceptable, usage. For example, one of the universal principles of standard English today is that when two negative words or prefixes are used together, the first negates the second, making the whole expression positive, just as in mathematics. The meaning of "He didn't say nothing" is "He said something," more or less. Yet in Shakespeare's time the "mathematical" principle did not always hold; a second negative could merely strengthen the first. (The same is true in much colloquial usage today.) The grammatical principles of standard English – indeed, of every language known to man – are always changing; and at every time there will always be some confusion and disagreement over standard forms. See **kind(s) of** or **who, whom** in VOCABULARY for examples of this.

In order to discourse on how language works, we need some specialized grammatical terms. The rest of this chapter looks at the most essential of these, as well as at some of the more general grammatical principles of standard English.

Sentence Structure

Let's start with a sentence.

Fritz has mitts.

We say *Fritz* is the subject of this sentence. This is a way of showing where the word "Fritz" comes in the sentence, and how it affects the other words. The words which are most commonly used as subjects are called **nouns**.

The subject of a sentence is always linked to a **predicate**. This term likewise has to do only with how the word works in a sentence. Predicates are always **verbs**. In this case, *has* is the verb that functions in this sentence as the predicate. Every complete English sentence has a predicate.

What about *mitts*, then? This is another noun, but it is affected by the verb in a way that the subject noun is not. (The mitts would be quite unrecognizable if, for example, *chews up* or *destroys* were the predicate.) We call *mitts* the object of the predicate *has*.

The usual order of **declarative** English **sentences**, or statements, is SUBJECT + PREDICATE (+ OBJECT). In **interrogative sentences** (questions), part or all of the predicate may come ahead of the subject, as in "Have you tried that key?" In **negative** sentences, *not* or some other negative is inserted within the predicate, as in "You have not tried that key." So the order of the words in the sentence, its **syntax**, itself conveys meaning beyond the dictionary meanings of the separate words.

Parts of Speech

We've already seen that only verbs may function as predicates in a sentence. A verb such as *wears* needs an object. We call this a **transitive** verb. (Think of a transit running from the verb to an object.) In "Fritz wears mitts," *wears* is a transitive verb. "Fritz wears" by itself does not make sense. On the other hand, the verb in "Fritz snored" doesn't need an object. We call this kind of verb **intransitive**. Transitive verbs are the movers, and intransitive verbs the doers of our language. All action and reaction in a sentence come from their interplay and the contribution of their meaning.

Transitive verbs have two forms, **active** and **passive voice**. In the sentence

Fritz eyed the cat

the voice of the verb, *eyed*, is active: the subject acts on the verb which acts upon the object. We may recast the verb and the sentence in passive form:

The cat was eyed by Fritz,

which reverses the whole thing. Now the subject (*the cat*) is acted upon by the object (*Fritz*).

Transitive and intransitive verbs are commonly called **lexical** verbs because they communicate specific meaning of the sort that may be looked up in a dictionary or other lexicon (wordlist). Two other sorts of verb are called **grammatical** because their role is to change the grammatical, rather than the semantic, sense of other words in a sentence. The first of these is the **linking verb**: it links the adjective which comes after it to the noun which went before it.

Fritz *is* old. Fritz *looks* tired. Fritz *seems* happy.

Each of these linking verbs has the effect of referring the adjective which follows (the **complement**) to the subject, *Fritz.*

The other type of grammatical verb is the **auxiliary verb**, which modifies the effect of a lexical verb with which it is used.

She *hadn't* seen him. You *will* write. I *am going* to do it. *Do* you have it?

The most common auxiliary verbs in English are *be* and *have*. *Be* is also the most irregular verb in our language.

The grammatical role of a verb may change. If you add *-ing* to it, it may be used as a noun. In the sentence "I love flying and parties," "flying" and "parties" both function as nouns. This kind of verb-noun formation is called a **gerund** (pronounced "jerrend" to rhyme with "errand").

Another verb form, the **present participle**, also ends in *-ing*, which can cause confusion. A gerund and a present participle may look alike, but the first functions as a noun, the second as an adjective. In

They are showering themselves

are is a linking verb, and *showering* a present participle, acting as an adjective. In effect, *showering themselves* is the complement of the subject, *they.*

You must be sure whether you intend to use a gerund or a present participle, as the meaning of your sentence may be greatly affected by an incorrect choice:

I'd like to see his writing (gerund).
I'd like to see him writing (present participle).

In the first of these sentences *writing* is a noun: his books, his letters, his written output. In the second, *writing* is an adjective: *him writing* means the man writing.

Verbs also have **past participle** forms. These commonly end in *-ed*, and are often used with an auxiliary verb. For example, in

I have loved many

the word *loved* is a past participle, used here with the auxiliary verb *have*. Verbs which add *-ed* to form the first person past and the past participle are called **regular verbs**. Verbs which form these parts in some other way are called **irregular verbs**. (Under **irregular verbs** I include what grammarians call "strong" verbs, verbs such as *lie, lay, lain*, as well as truly irregular verbs such as *be*.) A list of the principal parts of the most common irregular verbs is on the inside back cover.

A verb shows the relationship of its subject to time past, present, future, or hypothetical. It does this through its **tense** and **mood**. Let's look at the regular verb *hammer*. We begin by listing its **principal parts**:

hammer (infinitive)
hammered (simple past)
hammered (past participle)

INDICATIVE MOOD
  PRESENT
    I hammer (habitual), I am hammering (progressive), I do
      hammer (emphatic)
    do I hammer (interrogative habitual)? am I hammering
      (interrogative progressive)?
    I do not hammer (negative habitual), I am not hammering
      (negative progressive)

  FUTURE
    I shall/will hammer (See VOCABULARY, under **shall, will**)
    I am going to hammer
    shall/will I hammer?   I shall/will not hammer
    am I going to hammer?   I am not going to hammer

  PAST
    I hammered (simple), I have hammered (compound), I did
      hammer (emphatic)

I was hammering, I used to hammer (both imperfect)
I had hammered (pluperfect)
I should/would have hammered (conditional)
I shall/will have hammered (future)

did I hammer?	I didn't hammer,
have I hammered?	I haven't hammered
was I hammering?	I wasn't hammering
did I use to hammer?	I didn't use to hammer
(Formal: used I to hammer?)	(Formal: I used not to hammer)

IMPERATIVE MOOD

2nd person: hammer, you will hammer. Other: Let me (him, her, it, us, them) hammer.

SUBJUNCTIVE MOOD (See VOCABULARY, under **was**, **were**)
if I (he, she, it) were sure (subjunctive)
if I (he, she, it) were not sure (negative subjunctive)

One of the difficult aspects of English, especially for someone learning it as a foreign language, is learning its many irregular verbs. Foreign students usually learn them in lists: *buy*, *bought*, *bought*, *ride*, *rode*, *ridden*, and *split*, *split*, *split* are examples. English-speaking children unconsciously absorb many of these through schooling and everyday conversation—but even native adults habitually confuse the principal parts of such commonplace irregular verbs as *lie*, *lay*, *lain* and *lay*, *laid*, *laid*. (See VOCABULARY, under **lay**, **lie**.) American usage may treat a verb as irregular where British treats it as regular (Amer. colloquial *dove* versus Brit. *dived*), or vice versa (Amer. *bided* versus Brit. *bode*). Check your dictionary for further assistance with specific verbs.

The meaning of a verb may be affected by the presence of an **adverb**. The difference between *she smiled innocently* and *she smiled craftily* is essentially the difference between the meanings of the adverbs *innocently* and *craftily*. Adverbs give us further information about the state or action suggested by the verb.

Grammar

Most, but not all, adverbs, end in -*ly*. A test, if you're in doubt about whether a certain word is functioning as an adverb, is to substitute an -*ly* adverb and compare its effect with that of the word in question. For example, if we are curious about the word *well* in "She sang well," we can see that an adverb such as *beautifully* functions similarly in the same position: "She sang beautifully." *Well* in this sentence must be an adverb.

Certain words change, or modify, nouns. We call these **adjectives**. In

A married man will stay at home

married is a **descriptive adjective**; it describes the noun it modifies. Most descriptive adjectives have three degrees of comparison:

I believe he is *happy* (positive).
I believe he is *happier* (or *more happy*) (comparative).
I believe he is *happiest* (or *(the) most happy*) (superlative).

The comparative degree is used to compare two things. In standard English the superlative degree is used only when three or more things are in the group under discussion. The forms *more [adjective]* and *(the) most [adjective]* are normally used only when the adjective has two or more syllables; they are also used to compare adverbs: *more happily, (the) most happily*. Note that *y* endings usually change to *ier* and *iest*, and that final consonants are often doubled: *fit, fitter, fittest* or *big, bigger, biggest*. We use the words *less* and *least* instead of *more* and *most* to indicate negative degrees: *less happy, (the) least happy*. The most common adjective in English, *good*, has the most irregular degrees: *better* (comparative) and *best* (superlative), *less good* (negative comparative), and *least good* (negative superlative). Other common irregular groups are *bad, worse, worst, little, less, least*, and *much/many, more, most*.

Apart from descriptive adjectives, we have various kinds of **limiting adjectives**. These include the **definite article** (*the*), the **indefinite articles** (*a, an*), and the **possessive adjectives** (*my,* *your, his, her, its, our, their*). **Interrogative**, **relative**, and **indefinite pronouns** may also function as limiting adjectives.

Interrogative: *Which* (adjective) cup do you prefer? *Which* (pronoun) do you prefer?

Relative: He may visit *what* (adjective) friends he likes. He may do *what* (pronoun) he likes.

Indefinite: *Many* (adjective) immigrants are growing dissatisfied. *Many* (pronoun) are growing dissatisfied.

Numbers usually function as adjectives. **Cardinal numbers** tell how many: *one, two, three*, and so on. **Ordinal numbers** tell in what order things come: *first, second, third*, and so forth.

Possessive nouns usually function as adjectives in a sentence. In English, the possessive case is often made by adding an apostrophe and *s* to the noun: *winter's end, boys' games*, or with the construction **the** [noun] **of** [noun]: *the end of winter, the games of boys*. For more information see TYPOGRAPHY, under **apostrophe**.

Adjectives themselves are modified by adverbs. In the sentence

A happily married man won't bother to wander,

the adverb *happily* modifies the adjective *married*. As was noted above, most adverbs are formed by adding *-ly*, which adds the meaning of "in a [adjective] way" to the adjective.

Nouns may have **singular** (one) or **plural** (more than one) forms, or both. The plural of most English nouns is made by adding *-s* or *-es* to the singular:

rose, roses   tea, teas   Knox, the Knoxes

Some plurals, such as *child, children, foot, feet, man, men, ox, oxen*, and *woman, women*, are irregular. Nouns which have singular and plural forms are called **countable nouns**. Nouns such as *rice* and *air*, which do not, are called **non-countable** nouns (or **mass nouns**).

Abstract nouns name things that have no material existence: *pity, love, strength, poverty*. All other nouns are called **concrete**. **Proper nouns** name a particular person or thing: *Steve Biko*,

Grammar

the Mississippi River, Auckland. In English, unlike ordinary (or **common**) nouns, proper nouns always begin with a capital letter. (See TYPOGRAPHY, under **capitals**.)

It was a real *tragedy* (abstract/common).
The dominant religion in Bali is *Buddhism*
  (abstract/proper).
He bought a new *car* (concrete/common).
I lent the ladder to *Larry* (concrete/proper).

Nouns, adjectives, verbs, and adverbs are all lexical words. But nouns may be replaced by a class of non-lexical, or **grammatical**, words called **pronouns**. A pronoun is a non-lexical substitute for an understood lexical noun. Its meaning depends entirely on what has preceded it.

That red-haired man over there is leaving. *He* is leaving.

Here the lexical noun-phrase *that red-haired man over there* is replaced by the third person singular pronoun *he*.

The verb ending is affected by the number and person of the subject noun or pronoun. For example, the present tense of the verb *hammer* is:

Pronoun	Verb forms		Grammatical name of form
I	hammer,	am hammering, do hammer	(first person singular)
thou	hammerest,	art hammering, dost hammer	(second person singular)*
he/she/it	hammers,	is hammering, does hammer	(third person singular)
we	hammer,	are hammering, do hammer	(first person plural)
you	hammer,	are hammering, do hammer	(second person plural)
they	hammer,	are hammering, do hammer	(third person plural)

* Not used in modern standard English. The second person plural pronoun and verb forms are now used for both singular and plural subjects.

In English, **personal pronouns** have differing forms to show if they are being used as a subject (*I* ate supper), an object (the tree fell on *me*), or as a possessive pronoun (*mine* was the biggest). The **possessive adjective** forms, used in noun-phrases such as "*My* former employer died," or "*Whose* business is that?" are related to personal pronouns, but they function as adjectives.

Subject	Object	Possessive pronoun	Possessive adjective
I	me	mine	my
[thou	thee	thine	thy]
he	him	his	his
she	her	hers	her
it	it	its	its
who	whom	whose	whose
we	us	ours	our
you	you	yours	your
they	them	theirs	their

In English the subject and the main verb must agree in person and number. For example, the third person singular pronoun requires the third person singular verb ending. First decide whether the subject is singular or plural, then be sure to use the corresponding form of the verb.

An agreement on rents and taxes *was* signed (singular subject, "agreement").

Rents and taxes *were* quite reasonable (plural subject, "rents and taxes").

There *is* a large herd of cows missing (singular subject, "herd").

The cattle *are* missing (plural subject, "cattle").

Demonstrative pronouns are words such as *this*, *that*, *these*, and *those*, which contrast the relation between two or more objects, a nearer and a farther.

This hat, the one I am holding, is yours; that one must be hers.

These dishes are all we need; put those away.

Indefinite pronouns are similar in effect to demonstrative pronouns but are not as specific. Words such as *each*, *many*, *none*, *few*, *all*, *some*, and *any* are examples. Most are also used as adjectives, and some also as nouns.

Many came to watch (pronoun). I called *many* times (adjective).
All was over (pronoun). It rained *all* night (adjective). He gave his *all* to the cause (noun).

Interrogative pronouns are used to ask questions about the object of a verb. These include *who*, *which*, and *what*.

Who is coming to dinner tonight? Who are these people? Which will arrive first? What will they be wearing?

Note that some interrogative words such as *how*, *when*, and *why* are actually adverbs, not pronouns, in that they refer to the way in which the verb acts, not to its object.

Relative pronouns either replace nouns or show the relation between words in a phrase. The words most commonly used as relative pronouns are *who*, *which*, *what*, and *that*. Note that *who* is used of persons, *which* and *that* of either persons or things, and *what* of things only. For examples, see VOCABU-LARY, under **that, what, which, who**.

A **preposition** is a word which usually, but not always, precedes a noun, showing the relation between that noun and other nouns in the sentence. This relation is often, but not always, one of physical space or time. Here are examples of some of the most common prepositions in everyday use:

up a tree	*down* the road	*in* the house
outside the door	*on* the table	*off* the wall
into the stew	*out of* the question	*over* the edge
under the volcano	*during* the war	*past* the corner
underneath the bed	*within* these walls	*because of* you
below the town	*beneath* the stone	*after* the fall

The noun or pronoun which follows the preposition is called the **object of the preposition**. The whole word-group (preposition + object) is called a **phrase**. Phrases usually function as adjectives or adverbs, occasionally as nouns.

He ran *from the city* (as an adverb qualifying *ran*).
The dog *from the city* killed a deer (as an adjective qualifying *dog*).
After ten is a good time to call (as a noun, subject of sentence).

The correct choice and placing of prepositions can be tricky, particularly if your native tongue is not English. One of the most common ways in which American and British diverge is in the use of prepositions. American will say, "Her office is on Windward Street," and British, "Her office is in Windward Street." There are many other examples of this. Be guided by your dictionary; also see DIALECTS.

Although prepositions usually come before their objects, it is perfectly acceptable to end a sentence with a preposition, especially if you can't think of a better way in which to put it.

What has he been up to?
This is the kind of nonsense I won't put up with.
(Non-S*: This is the kind of nonsense up with which I will not put (Winston S. Churchill).)

Prepositions, like nouns and verbs, are lexical, at least up to a point. Each preposition has a range of specific dictionary meanings. But, by contrast to other lexical words which have independent meanings (*tree*, for example), prepositions need objects (nouns) in order to convey a specific meaning. The word "from" on its own may give the impression of placing distance between two things, but for any specific meaning we need to know what the two things are, as in "*Jim* drove from *the city*."

Standard use of prepositions is not a simple thing. Many of the vocabulary problems listed in the next section are really

* The abbreviation 'Non-S' indicates non-standard usage. Churchill was, of course, joking.

preposition problems. For example, should we say *different to*, *different from*, or *different than*? (Look under **different** for help with that one.) If you've ever tried to learn another language, you'll know that it's not safe to assume you can always translate the words of an English phrase literally to convey the same meaning in the other language. Chances are your phrase won't be **idiomatic** (i.e. according to standard usage) in the other language. It's not as hard to learn separate words in another language as it is to learn its idiomatic expressions.

A **conjunction** is a word that joins other words, or grammatically linked groups of words, in a sentence. There are two types, **coordinating conjunctions**, and **subordinating conjunctions**. The first of these joins things of the same grammatical rank.

Jack *and* Jill (joining words) went up the hill.
He went up the hill *and* into the house (joining phrases).
He went up the hill *and* she went into the house (joining clauses).

(A **clause** is a group of words which is a grammatically complete sentence in that it usually has a subject and always a predicate but which forms part of a larger sentence.)

Other coordinating conjunctions are *as well as*, *but*, *whereas*, *either*, *or*, *else*, *neither*, *nor*, and *for*. Others, called **correlatives**, are used in pairs:

Both Jack *and* Jill went up the hill.
Not only Jack *but also* Jill went up the hill.
Either Jack *or* Jill went up the hill.
Neither Jack *nor* Jill went up the hill.

By contrast, **subordinating conjunctions** join clauses in such a way as to show that they are not equal: one depends on the other.

I went to church *because* she asked me to go.
Joan goes swimming *whenever* she has the chance.

The whole group [subordinating conjunction + clause] is

called a **subordinate clause**. A subordinate clause is grammatically complete (it usually has a subject and always a predicate), but because of the subordinating conjunction it is logically dependent on the independent clause attached to it.

Adverbs, pronouns, and nouns used adverbially may also be used as conjunctions to give a logical thread to a sequence of clauses, though the clauses may be separate sentences. A semicolon precedes the conjunction, which is then followed by a comma.

> He lost nearly everything; *however*, an old family Bible escaped the flames.
> I know you are tired. We must, *nevertheless*, continue the search.

See TYPOGRAPHY, under **semi-colon**, and VOCABULARY, under **however** (a very common adverbial conjunction).

A final class of words is the **interjection**, which is usually vocal and emotive in effect, and has no logical grammatical relation with anything else in the sentence. Some common examples are

> *Oh! Ah! Alas! Damn! My! Boo! Ouch!*

Grammatical Analysis

Now let's try to use these terms to communicate something about a real sentence.

> John and Jane eyed the doorman.

This is the standard syntax for a declarative sentence: SUBJECT (*John and Jane*) + PREDICATE (*eyed*) + OBJECT (*the doorman*). As we would expect, the subject and the object are nouns. *John* and *Jane* are concrete proper nouns (remember?) joined by a coordinating conjunction, *and*, and *the doorman* is a concrete common noun, preceded by the definite article, *the*: they eyed a specific doorman. The verb, *eyed*, is transitive, as it clearly requires an object, *the doorman*.

Another example:

Do you think he would come if I called him tonight?

The inversion of the declarative form of the verb shows that this is an interrogative sentence (i.e. question) made up of two clauses. The syntax of the clauses is PREDICATE (*do . . . think*, transitive verb) + SUBJECT (*you*, 2nd person personal pronoun) + OBJECT (*he would come*, 3rd person singular personal pronoun, and conditional form of *come*). This is followed by a CONJUNCTION (*if*, subordinating) and a second clause consisting, again, of SUBJECT (*I*, 1st person singular personal pronoun) + PREDICATE (*called*, past tense used to express hypothetical possibility, qualified by adverb, *tonight*) + OBJECT (*him*).

The underlying structures are quite predictable and not all that complex:

Declarative: SUBJECT + PREDICATE + OBJECT.

Interrogative: PREDICATE + SUBJECT + OBJECT + SUBORDINATE CONJUNCTION + SUBJECT + PREDICATE + OBJECT?

Before you get involved in the finer points of grammar in a sentence, try first to work out how it functions in terms of subject and predicate. A subject may be quite long, but once you realize that all those separate words are really functioning together as a single subject, things will seem a lot simpler. For example:

Taxation without representation, without even the hope of representation, was finally too much of a burden for the normally law-abiding citizens of Manor Flats

is really just SUBJECT + PREDICATE + OBJECT (complement). Try to get as simple an overview as you can before zeroing in on the details. Here the subject is a long one, *Taxation without representation, without even the hope of representation*, but is just a common noun (*taxation*) qualified by two adjectival phrases. The predicate is *was*, a linking verb, so the rest of the sentence is merely a complement of the subject. The lexical gist of the whole sentence could be represented by the formula Taxation = Burden.

It's hard to conceive of an everyday situation when so much grammatical information might be useful or interesting. It's really a specialist vocabulary, just like the technical terms of sailing, printing, or computer programming. In fact, all specialists have their own vocabularies of usually at least forty or fifty terms. (This is a minimum: doctors, engineers, and philosophers, for example, use hundreds.) They need them to be able to describe accurately their specialized knowledge, just as we need the terms of grammar in order to be able to talk about how language works. You don't use all the terms at once, but it helps to have some understanding of them.

I have put this chapter first because I use many of the terms discussed in it within the course of the rest of the book. This is the specialist vocabulary needed for discussing the workings of English.

If, while using the book later, you forget what a particular term means (it will usually be printed in bold type, e.g. **verb**), look in the Glossary of Grammatical Terms (pp. 167–80). Also, check the Index.

Vocabulary

This is an alphabetical list of the words underlying most common standard English usage problems. Grammatical terms that occur here are explained in the Glossary (pp. 167–80). For general information regarding distinctive American and British usages see DIALECTS (pp. 148–54). For information about spelling and pronunciation see your dictionary. For further guidance on general topics see Further Reading (pp. 181–5). The abbreviation Non-S indicates non-standard usage.

A

a, an Use **an** before nouns beginning with a vowel sound, regardless of spelling, **a** before all other nouns.

an official   an 80-year-old   an honorary colonel.

acute, chronic An **acute** problem is one which has come to a crisis and needs immediate attention. A **chronic** problem is one that has remained unchanged for some time.

adage means *old proverb*. Don't put "old" before it.

admit means *confess to* and needs no preposition.

He admits the crime.

(Non-S but common informally: He admits to the crime.)

adverse, averse The first means *strongly opposed* or *contrary*; the second, often used jokingly, means *somewhat opposed* or *reluctant*.

She is adverse to your suggestion that the money should be
borrowed.

I'm sure he wouldn't be averse to a little fun now and then.

affect, effect The first is a verb with two distinct meanings:
influence (this is a vague sense, and more precise wording
would be preferable) and *pretend*. The second, as a verb, means
bring about, accomplish. **Effect** is the usual noun form.

He was affected by the heat. (Better: The heat made him
irritable, tired, and so on.)

The official affected indifference to her pleas, though it was
obvious that he had been moved by them.

The burglar effected his entry with a crowbar.

Your complaints have finally had an effect.

affinity means *mutual attraction or relationship*. It is followed by
between or **with**.

Jane soon discovered an affinity with the family next door.

There is usually some affinity between parents with young
children.

afterward, afterwards The first is preferred in American
usage, the second in British. Either is acceptable in standard
English.

agenda is a singular noun in English. Its plural is **agendas**.

aggravate means *make worse*. It is often used loosely to mean
irritate or *annoy* (perhaps due to confusion with **exasperate**),
but this usage is, strictly speaking, non-standard.

Her pneumonia was aggravated by the failure of the heating
system.

(Non-S but common informally: I find Roger's eight-year-
old extremely aggravating.)

aggression, aggressiveness The first suggests physical

violence, the second merely assertiveness or boldness. The adjective for both is *aggressive*.

> The continual aggression of the school bully finally got the better of him.

> You'll have to use more verbal aggressiveness when you argue your case.

alleviate means *give temporary relief*. It implies that the underlying problem is still unresolved.

> The Council alleviated the chaos caused by the train strike by allowing cars to be parked in the city.

all right "Alright is alwrong," was the (written) comment of one of my teachers.

allude, elude The first means *refer indirectly*. It should not be used in direct reference. (The noun is **allusion,** not to be confused with **illusion.**) **Elude** is an altogether different word which means *escape from*.

> When she spoke of dark doings, she must have been alluding to the former President's crimes.

> The family motto was an allusion to their prowess on twenty-two medieval battlefields.

> It took Goldilocks little time to elude her pursuers.

> The thief was too elusive for them.

along with, together with If either of these is used in a construction such as "X, along (or together) with Y," the verb agrees with X alone.

> The farmer, along with most of his workers, expects [singular] a good harvest.

alternate, alternative The first means *every other one*. The second means *another choice*.

> The flag had alternate [or alternating] stripes of red and green.

> The alternative is to leave now and send the money later.

Strict usage dictates that there can be no more than two alternatives (Latin *alter*, "either of two"), though this is widely ignored, especially in informal conversation.

although, though The two are virtually interchangeable, except that the first never occurs at the end of a sentence, or after **as** or **even**.
>She felt tired, although she had slept all afternoon.
>She felt tired, though she had slept all afternoon.
>She felt tired. She had slept all afternoon, though.
>She looked as though she were tired, even though she had slept all afternoon.

altogether is an adverb meaning *completely*. The spelling **all together** shows that **all** and **together** are to be considered as two separate adverbs.
>I think she had better forget it altogether.
>The children were all together in the middle of the park.

amend, emend The first, a verb, means *improve*. The second, also a verb, means *revise, correct*. The nouns are **amendment** and **emendation**.
>You had better try to amend your manners, my boy.
>I spent three days emending the manuscript and four retyping it.

amid(st), among(st) The first is used with nouns which denote non-countable masses, the second with things that can be counted. The -st endings have a somewhat old-fashioned ring today, though they are still acceptable standard English.
>Amid the debris we found two survivors.
>There was her ring, lying among the nuts and washers.

among, between The first is usually associated with a group of more than two members. **Between** is normally limited to groups of no more than two, but may be used of larger groups, provided their members are considered as individuals.

amoral, immoral

We divided the pie between the two children (group of two).
Share the water among the crowd (group larger than two).
Relations between the four unions were excellent (independently acting groups).

amoral, immoral The first means *independent of morality*, the second *evil in the eyes of society*.
Cats are obviously quite amoral creatures.
He resigned after a jury found him guilty of committing immoral acts.

ancient means *of times long past* (specifically, before the fall of the Roman Empire). Its use as meaning *antiquated* or *old* is informal and usually jocular.

and/or This construction is unacceptable in standard English. One or other of the two words is usually enough. If not, rewrite the sentence.

another suggests something else of equal nature or size.
Kanamoto has contributed another 5,000 yen to the strike fund [implies 5,000 yen had already been given].
Kanamoto contributed a further 5,000 yen to the strike fund [implies an indeterminate amount had already been given].

anticipate means *take suitable action in the light of advance knowledge or information*. It is not the same as **expect** or **guess**.
She anticipated the summer heat by moving to the beach.

anxious has connotations of worry or apprehension. It may mean simply *keenly eager*, but only in an informal context.
I'm anxious that he may not be able to find the key.
(Non-S but common informally: I'm anxious to visit the new jazz club in Springfield.)

anybody, anyone Each of these pronouns requires a singular verb. Spell as two separate words only when the second is emphasized.

Has anybody come forward to claim the prize?

We have the murderer, but haven't found any body yet.

Anyone who likes dogs is welcome in her house.

There are five wines on the list, but any one will do.

any more Always spelled as two words.

anyone See **anybody**.

anything, anywhere Always spelled as single words.

anytime, at any time The first is standard American, the second standard British.

American: Call on him anytime you like.

British: Call on him at any time you like.

anyway Spell as one word when used as an adverb, as two when used as adjective (any) + noun (way).

I'll plan on seeing him tomorrow anyway.

The trapped insect couldn't find any way out of the bottle.

appraise, apprise The first of these verbs means *assess, evaluate*, the second *inform*.

Can a father appraise his son's life objectively?

The unflappable hostess quietly apprised him of the state of his trousers.

approve, approve of The first means *authorize*, the second *judge to be good*. The second meaning requires the preposition **of**.

Anyone approved by the committee may park there.

I cannot approve of such dishonesty.

apt to, liable to, likely to, prone to All denote probability. Both **likely to** and **liable to** denote particular situations, with the second usually having an added unpleasant connotation. In contrast, **apt to** and **prone to** denote general or habitual situations, with, once again, the second having a negative connotation.

> He is likely to see her before he gets back this evening [particular].
>
> Your friend is liable to get hurt unless he stops carrying on like that [particular, unpleasant].
>
> The mountain air is apt to turn cool after seven o'clock [habitual].
>
> He's prone to asthma attacks in August [habitual, unpleasant].

arbitrate means *judge or give a decision in a dispute*. It is sometimes confused with **mediate**, which means *act as a go-between in a dispute*. The two functions are not the same.

aroma refers to pleasant smells only.

artiste means some sort of public entertainer or performer. The spelling is the same for either sex.

as, like When **as** means *similar to (and including)* there should be a verb in what follows. If there is only a noun or pronoun, use **like** instead. Do not use **like** as a substitute for **as if**. See also **like**.

> Do as you always do.
>
> (Non-S: Do like you always do.)
>
> You did it like a veteran.
>
> It seemed as if he'd had enough.
>
> (Non-S: It seemed like he'd had enough.)

as if, as though Use a past tense (Brit.) or subjunctive (Amer.) form of the verb that follows either of these phrases if you want to convey the idea of something unlikely or impossible. Use a present tense verb to convey the idea of possibility.

British: He talks as if he was the emperor himself [past tense = impossibility].

American: He talks as if he were the emperor himself [subjunctive = impossibility].

He talks as if he is the emperor himself [present tense = possibility].

as to whether Omit the first two words.

as yet Omit the first word.

attain means *achieve*, *accomplish* and has positive connotations. It is not a synonym of **reach**.

auspicious means *promising*, *of good omen*. It is not a synonym of **special** or **memorable**.

avenge, revenge The first verb conveys the idea of seeking a fair settlement, an equal recompense for some wrong. The second implies an overriding and overwhelming desire for personal satisfaction, and has much stronger emotional connotations. The noun form of the first is **vengeance**, while that of the second is **revenge**. See also **revenge for, on**.

average, mean, median The first two are synonyms. In arithmetic, an **average** is the sum of a group of quantities divided by the number of quantities in that group. The average of 4, 9, and 20 is $4 + 9 + 20 = 33 \div 3 = 11$. The **mid-range** of this series is the value exactly halfway between the highest and the lowest number of the series: the mid-range here is 12. The **median** is the middle number of the actual series: 9. **Average** may also be used loosely to mean *normal, usual, unexceptional*; but the other two terms should be avoided except in technical writing. Note that the term "average income" in common nontechnical writing almost always means median income.

awake, awaken The principal parts and meanings of these

verbs have been considerably confused over time. The past tense and past participle forms of the first are **awoke, awaked** and of the second **awakened, awoken**. The mix-up is caused by the fact that two different Old English verbs have merged their senses into one. American and British usage vary in their preferences; check your dictionary for further guidance.

That morning I awoke [or awakened] him later than usual.

She has obviously awaked [or awoken] new desires and longings in him.

aware requires, in formal usage, the preposition *of* and an object. Informally only, it may be treated as a simple adjective.

Are you aware of the disturbance you are causing?

(Non-S but common informally: He's a pretty aware kind of person.)

awhile, a while The preposition **for** precedes only the second of these.

Sit down and rest awhile. Sit down and rest for a while.

B

backward, backwards The first is preferred in American usage, the second in British. Either is acceptable in standard English.

bacteria is a plural noun. (The singular is **bacterium**.)

bad, badly The first is an adjective, the second an adverb. Both have many different meanings, which you will find listed in your dictionary. Their antonyms are **good** and **well**. For examples see **good**.

bait, bate A hook is baited; breath is bated (held back).

barbaric, barbarous The first has to do with the historic customs, dress, and characteristics of primitive or supposedly uncivilized people (think of "barracks"). The second is purely pejorative, suggesting cruel or sadistic behaviour (think of "barbed wire"), and may be used in a modern context.

That evening the huntsmen were treated to a barbaric feast.
The colonel's guards committed many barbarous acts.

basically An overused and generally unnecessary word.

bereft means *bereaved, deprived of someone or something*. It does not mean merely *without*.

beside, besides The first means *next to*, the second, *in addition to*. **Besides** does not mean *other than*.

Beside him on the table was his trusty knife.
Besides English and French I am studying music and geography this year.
(Non-S: He must have started the car with something besides the key.)

between See **among**.

between you and me This is correct. "Between you and I" is not. (For further explanation, see GRAMMAR, p. 21.)

bi-, semi- Take care when using these prefixes with units of time:

biannual = twice a year
biennial = every two years
semi-monthly = twice a month
semi-weekly = twice a week

The word "bi-monthly" is ambiguous, meaning either *every two months* OR *twice a month*, and should always be avoided. "Bi-weekly" presents the same problem. Use "every two months" or "every two weeks" instead.

billion A British billion is a million million; an American billion is a thousand million. An American trillion is the same as a British billion. Most of us use these terms vaguely anyway, but mathematicians, physicists, statisticians and economists should be aware of the possibility of transatlantic confusion.

blatant means *obvious*.
   This is most blatant flattery—but do go on!

born, borne Both are past participles of the verb *bear*. **Born** is used only in the context of birth. **Borne** is the past participle of **bear** in the sense of *put up with, stand*, but it also can be used, either actively or passively, to mean *give birth to*.
   Michel's godfather was born on Bastille Day, 1900.
   Such suffering and pain could scarcely be borne, she
      thought.
   By her fortieth birthday she had borne twelve children.
   Not one of the sons borne by her lives in that town.

both should be limited to two things, and not used where **each** is called for. See also **either**.
   He is pure in thought, word, and deed.
   (Non-S: He is pure, both in thought, word, and deed.)
   There was a sandy beach on each side of the river.
   (Non-S: There was a sandy beach on both sides of the river.)

bottom line A trendy and overworked phrase which usually refers to the essential condition in an agreement or the ultimate meaning of something. It may eventually come to be regarded as acceptable in a serious or formal context, but for the present it is not.

breach, breech, breeches The first, as noun, means *gap* or *infraction*, the second means *rear, lower part. Breeches* are pants; the spelling "britches" in Amer. colloquial writing more accurately conveys the actual standard pronunciation of the word.
   His treatment of the hostess was a grave breach of etiquette.

The breech is the part of a gun which lies behind its barrel.
The trouble with their marriage was that she was too big for
his breeches.

burgeoning means *budding*, *sprouting*, so should be used of
something which is just beginning to grow. It does not mean
merely *continuing to grow*.

but . . . however, but . . . on the other hand Each one separately indicates a change of direction, so only one should be
used in a sentence.
But that was an older woman. That was an older woman,
however.
(Non-S: But that was an older woman, however.)
But he still had the map. On the other hand, he still had the
map.
(Non-S: But, on the other hand, he still had the map.)

C

can, may The first refers to what is possible or able to be accomplished, the second to what is acceptable or permissible. The
past tense of *can* is *could*; that of *may* is *might*.
Man can fly with mechanical assistance.
You may not leave until after the ambassador has departed.

careen, career These two verbs are often confused. The first
means *tip at an angle* (ships are careened so barnacles can be
scraped off their hulls). The second means *move at top speed,
rush wildly*. Informally, especially in the USA, **careen** is commonly used in place of **career**.
The truck careered straight down the hill and into the barn.
(Non-S but common informally: The truck careened
straight down the hill and into the barn.)

case often adds nothing to a sentence.

In case of emergency, phone this number.

Better: In an emergency, phone this number.

It has often been the case that keys have been lost.

Better: Keys have often been lost.

celebrant, celebrator The first is a participant in a religious ceremony; the second refers to anyone taking part in some kind of celebration.

The abbot will preside as celebrant at the requiem mass.

More than six hundred celebrators turned up at the victory party.

celibate means *unmarried*. It does not necessarily mean *chaste*.

censor, censure The first, as a verb, refers to the suppression of part of a book, letter, or other piece of writing for political or moral reasons; as a noun **censor** refers to the official who does this. The verb **censure** means *condemn, criticize harshly*; as a noun it means *condemnation, harsh criticism*.

Much of the letter had been heavily censored, and what remained made little sense to her.

The government was defeated by an opposition censure motion.

character is often used to turn an adjective into an abstract noun. Avoid this wherever possible by using the relevant noun.

The intense character of her speech won us all over.

Better: The intensity of her speech won us all over.

choose between This verb should be used with the conjunction *and*, not *or*.

You will have to choose between being a financial success and being happy with yourself.

(Non-S: You will have to choose between being a success or being happy.)

chord, cord The first is a specialist (geometrical and zoological) term; in musical terminology it refers to two or more musical notes sounding at once. A cord may be a thick string (or, in anatomy, anything string-like), an electrical cable, or a measure of wood cut for fire or pulp.

Long-sustained chords can strain a choir's vocal cords.

chronic means *lasting a long time* (it is related to the Greek word *chronos*, time); its opposite is **acute.**

Many parts of Africa have suffered from a chronic shortage of food.

collectible is the preferred spelling, though "collectable" is also acceptable. Be consistent.

collide, collision should be used only when two moving objects come together. A car does not collide with a wall, it runs into it.

comic, comical Something comic is meant to be funny; a comical thing was not planned to draw laughs—which is why it does.

common as adjective means *belonging equally to more than one*. See also **mutual**.

comparatively Avoid this word unless a stated comparison is made. See also **relatively**.

Following the successes of the first three days, comparatively little was achieved on Thursday.

(Non-S: Comparatively little ground has been covered so far.)

compare to, with Use **to** when comparing two unlike things, **with** when comparing two similar things. The same applies to the adjective **comparable** and the noun **comparison**.

Shall I compare thee to a summer's day [unlike objects]?

Was his love really comparable to a summer's day?

41

compendium

How does last year's model compare with this year's [similar objects]?

Could you make a comparison of last year's model with this year's?

compendium refers to a summary or abridgement, not an all-inclusive work. The plural is **compendiums** or **compendia**.

complacent, complaisant The first means *self-satisfied*, *smugly content*. The second means *eager to please*.

I can't stand his complacent attitude.

He seems a likable and complaisant lad; he should go far.

compose, comprise The first means *constitute, make up*. It may be either active or passive. The parts compose the whole, not vice versa.

Ten provinces and two territories compose Canada.

Canada is composed of ten provinces and two territories.

Comprise is the converse of **compose**. Its active form means *consist of*, and its passive form, which must be followed by *in*, means *be comprehended*. The whole always comprises the parts.

Canada comprises ten provinces and two territories.

Ten provinces and two territories are comprised in Canada.

conceived The preceding adverbs in expressions such as *first conceived*, *initially conceived*, and *originally conceived* are unnecessary and should be left out.

concept refers to a general idea derived from specific instances. Do not use as a loose synonym for *idea*.

Gradually the concept of Romanticism began to dominate the Western artistic world.

conform may be followed by either *to* or *with*.

Club members must conform to our standards of dress.

Should a wife conform with her husband's political views?

connote, denote The former refers to the associative overtones of a word; the latter is limited to its dictionary definition.

The word "luxury" connotes extravagance and excess.

"Luxury" denotes the use of the best and most costly things necessary for the greatest pleasure and comfort.

consensus Avoid the expressions *general consensus* or *consensus of opinion*: the idea of general opinion is already contained in *consensus*. Note the spelling: it is related to *consent*, not *census*.

consequence is used of something which follows as the result of something else. The adjective is **consequent**, the adverb **consequently**. (Note: **consequential** has a more specialized meaning, *following as an indirect result*, and is not commonly used. **Inconsequential**, meaning *of little importance*, is a useful word, however.)

The consequence of our having the same surname was that we sat together at all the lectures.

In his youth he had bought an original Picasso print for an inconsequential sum.

consider does not require any preposition when used to mean *judge*, but is followed by the preposition **as** when meaning *discussed* or *examined*.

I consider him to be a fool.

The book considers Schweitzer as musicologist, physician, and theologian.

consist in, consist of The first means *have as its essential quality*, the second, *be made up*.

History does not consist only in annals of victory and defeat.

The pads of a dog's paw consist of many tough hairs.

contagious refers to diseases that are communicated through direct physical contact.

continual, continuous The first means *very frequent*, the second, *connected, unbroken, uninterrupted*.

I'm tired of these continual interruptions.

They have been drilling continuously for three days.

continuance, continuation The first means *going on existing* and is used intransitively. The second, much more commonly used, means *resuming, keeping up*, and is used transitively.

Do you believe there is some sort of continuance after death?

The next morning saw a continuation of their campaign for higher wages.

continuous See **continual**.

contrary, converse The first contradicts something, the second reverses its elements. The contrary of "The dog bit the man" is "The dog did not bite the man." The converse is "The man bit the dog." **Converse** is also used as a term in logic: the converse of the theorem *if a then b* is *if b then a*.

convince, persuade The first, meaning *cause to believe*, is followed by the preposition **that**. The second, meaning *lead to act*, is followed by the preposition **to**.

I soon convinced him that his son had not committed the crime.

Can you persuade her to come with us on Saturday?

cord See **chord**.

country, nation The first refers to geographical entities, the second to political and social ones.

The USSR is the largest country in the world.

Canada is a nation of two dominant cultures.

credible, credulous The first means *capable of being believed*, the second means *too ready to believe*.

Her story seemed very credible to me at the time.

He could always find some credulous soul to advance him some cash for a few hours.

crescendo is a musical term meaning *increasing (in volume of sound)*. It is often used as though it meant *climax* or *peak*, but this is incorrect.

After a fifteen-minute crescendo of wind and hail, a deafening clap of thunder shook the house.

(Non-S: The election campaign reached a crescendo on Saturday night.)

criteria is a plural noun. Its singular is **criterion**.

crucial means *decisive, critical*. It does not merely mean *important*.

The doctor explained that the crucial moment would come sometime on Sunday evening.

culminate means *reach a high point*. Do not use as a synonym for *conclude*.

His career culminated with the winning of the peace prize.

(Non-S: The evening culminated with the singing of the national anthem.)

current, currently As a synonym for *now* these words add little or nothing to the meaning of a sentence and should be replaced with something more precise.

D

dais, lectern, podium, rostrum A **dais** is a public platform large enough for several people; a **podium** holds only one. **Rostrum** describes a platform of any size. A **lectern** is not a platform at all, but a stand for holding reading material (lecture notes, music scores, speech text) before someone on a rostrum.

data This was originally a plural word (the singular is **datum**), and should still be treated as plural when the meaning is *collection of separate facts*. If it merely means *information* in a general sense, it may be treated as singular.

> The various data he had left on this sheet were [plural] altered during the night.
>
> Here is [singular] all the data we have on the subject of shoplifting.

decimate means *reduce by one-tenth*. It may be used to convey the idea of heavy loss, but not utter annihilation. The word has been overused, and is better avoided.

deduce, deduct The first of these verbs generally is used to mean *conclude from evidence*, but it has a more specific meaning in logic, explained under **deductive, inductive** below. **Deduct** means *subtract*.

> Holmes deduced that the soprano had been out for some time.
>
> The premiums for this insurance will be deducted from your wages.

deductive, inductive These logicians' terms are usually applied to the way in which an argument is presented. **Deductive** reasoning starts with the observation of general principles and then uses these principles to explain particular details. In the example above, if Holmes had already been informed that the soprano was not at home (general principle), he might have reasoned deductively that certain particular evidence of this would be manifest. If, on the other hand, he had had no advance knowledge of the soprano's whereabouts, he might have begun his reasoning with the observation of certain physical or otherwise external details, and then come to the conclusion that the lady must be out. This would be **inductive** reasoning. What Conan Doyle often calls deduction in the Sherlock Holmes stories is *actually* induction.

defective, deficient Something defective does not work properly; something deficient has something missing.

definite, definitive The first means *certain, precise,* the second, *complete, final.*
   Is it definite that you'll be away for eight days?
   He is working on the definitive biography of Paganini.

deplete, reduce The first means *exhaust, destroy,* and has negative connotations. The connotations of **reduce** are more neutral.
   The Secretary of the Interior's cronies have depleted the
      country's petroleum resources.
   Our stocks of vintage red were greatly reduced during the
      winter.

deplore means *lament, be regretful over,* and should refer to a thing, not a person. It has strong connotations of reproach or censure.
   We have always deplored her vanity. Her vanity is deplorable.
   (Non-S: We have always deplored her for her vanity.)

deprecate, depreciate The first means *express earnest (and often regretful) disapproval of,* the second *play down, belittle, be modest about,* and *reduce (a financial sum).*
   Art critics have generally deprecated this return to romanticism.
   Why do you continually depreciate your obvious talents?

diagnosis is an opinion about the nature of an illness or other problem based on observation of fact. See **prognosis**.

dialect, jargon, lingua franca The first refers to the form of a language spoken by any group of people which differs in some way from the standard form. All of us use some dialect or other when we converse informally with other members of our own group. (For convenience, this book groups all English dialects into two super-dialects, American and British.) **Jargon** refers to specialist dialect—the actual words and phrases peculiar to any group of surgeons, pilots, musicians, company presidents, writers, mechanics, society matrons, teachers, actors, farmers, children, and so forth. Jargon is not standard English; it is not intended for the public-at-large. The deliberate use of jargon outside the specialist group is as offensive as whispering to someone else in the company of a larger group. A **lingua franca** is an international language, one used in air travel, business communications, and scientific reports, for example, or between different linguistic groups within a single country, such as India. Standard English is the leading lingua franca of the world today—one of the many reasons it is worth mastering.

dice is generally acceptable as either a singular or a plural. Tradition insists, however, that "die" is the singular form.

differ, diverge Diverge is the opposite of **converge** and means *move apart*. It is not quite the same as differ. Differing opinions may be reconciled; in divergent ones the gap grows steadily wider.

different Often quite unnecessary, as in "She translated fifteen different Shakespeare plays into Russian."

different from, different to Although English usage experts since Fowler have stated that either is equally correct, many ordinary users of English have a gut feeling (on a basis of logic) that **different to** is wrong—difference implies divergence away *from* something else. It may be as well, therefore, to use **different from**.

> Your sense of the word is different from that of common usage.
>
> His argument is different to mine.

different than, differently than The latter is adverbial, meaning *in a different way*. **Different than** may be used informally in place of **different from** or **different to**, but this should be avoided in standard English.

He swims differently than his brother (does).

(Non-S: His brother looks different than him.)

dilemma describes a situation when there are only two (or, more loosely, several) courses of action open and each of them is clearly unsatisfactory. It is not a synonym for "problem" or "difficulty": a dilemma cannot be solved satisfactorily.

disassemble, dissemble The first means *take apart* (the opposite of **assemble**). The second means *conceal, disguise, pretend*.

They had to disassemble the yacht to get it out of the shed.

At first the intruder dissembled innocence with great success.

disassociate, dissociate Either form is acceptable. Pompous.

discreet, discrete The first means *careful, cautious, showing good judgement*. The second, a scientific term, means *separate, unconnected*.

As dawn approached she fell discreetly silent.

You should end up with a series of discrete random numbers.

disingenuous means *falsely ingenuous, not obviously crafty*. See also **ingenuous, ingenious.**

disinterested, uninterested The first means *impartial, neutral, not personally involved*. The second means *not interested*.

Is he sufficiently disinterested to make a good judge?

Malcolm is completely uninterested in any type of sport.

disposal, disposition The first originally meant *ordering, regulating, settling*, but recently it has taken on a more common

dissemble

meaning: *ridding oneself.* **Disposition** may be a synonym for *deployment* or *arrangement,* or it may mean *frame of mind.*

> We now have to solve the problem of the disposal of wastes from this plant.
> They met to plan the disposition of the eight battalions before the attack.
> Most mornings Kate had a sunny disposition, but by five in the afternoon she could become a termagant.

dissemble See **disassemble**.

dissociate See **disassociate**.

distinct, distinctive The first means *individual, separate,* the second, *special, unique.*

> Over the roar of the storm I could hear a distinct knock.
> His knock was quite distinctive: two shorts and a long.

diverge See **differ**.

divided into Use carefully: it is not a synonym for *composed of.*

> Gaul was divided into three parts.
> (Non-S: The coast was divided into cliffs and beaches.)

doubt as a verb is followed by **that** if the context is negative or a question, otherwise by **if** or **whether** (never by **but**).

> I don't doubt that we can weather the storm [not "doubt but that"].
> Was there ever any doubt that she would sing tonight?
> I doubt if we'll see much more of that scoundrel.
> She doubted whether he appreciated the seriousness of the crime.

doubtless(ly), undoubtedly The first of these suggests a kind of grudging (and perhaps faintly ironic) concession, the second conveys wholehearted acceptance of something. (In the first an -ly ending is sometimes added, but is unnecessary.)

"You doubtless know best," sighed the major, gloomily replacing the decanter.

He is undoubtedly the only Swahili speaker in the village.

due to used strictly means *caused by* or *attributable to*, but it is also used colloquially to mean *because of* or *owing to*.

The lay-offs were due to financial mismanagement.

(Non-S but acceptable colloquially: We arrived late due to a tree which had fallen across the road.)

E

each When **each** precedes the noun to which it refers, the verb should be singular. When it follows the noun the verb should be plural.

Each of the teachers has had time to look at the papers by now.

"Pot luck" means guests are each asked to bring a dish.

each and every An overworked phrase.

economic, economical The first is a specialist adjective, *having to do with the study of economics*. The second, meaning *cheap*, *thrifty*, is more common in everyday usage.

The government's economic policy is in shreds and tatters.

Living economically is no hardship, if you stop to think about it.

effect is a verb meaning *cause to happen* and a noun meaning *result*. See also **affect**.

She was hoping to effect a marriage with the man next door.

What is the effect of tobacco smoke on babies?

e.g. is an abbreviation of Latin *exempli gratia* and means *for* *example*. It is usually preceded by a comma, with a comma following each of the examples given. Use of such Latinisms bestows a certain antiquarian or pedantic effect on writing: beware!

> Many rare breeds, e.g. Saluki, Lhasa, and Chinese Chihuahua, were represented at the show.

egoism, egotism The first is a fairly neutral philosophical term meaning *self-interest*. The second is more pejorative, meaning *obsessively talking or thinking about oneself*.

> In contrast to his brother's altruistic bent, Perry's instinct for self-preservation showed true egoism.

> The egotism of that petty-minded and thoroughly spoiled brat turns my stomach.

either has two meanings: *one or other (but not both) of the two*, and *each of the two*.

> Either come in or go out.

> Lockers were lined up along either side of the hall.

eke You eke out a supply either by adding to it little by little, or by using it up carefully.

> She eked out her diet of oats with apples and new-laid eggs.

elder, eldest The first is a general term meaning *earlier born of two*. The second means *first-born* and is used only within the context of some kind of family group.

> Tomkins is the elder clerk now that Briggs has retired.

> I hadn't seen Peter, my eldest son, for over ten years.

elude means *escape from*. See also **allude**.

emend means *revise*. See also **amend**.

endemic, epidemic Both are used to describe human diseases. The first means the disease is to be found in a particular group

of people or a specific geographical area; the second describes an outbreak, often contagious. See also **contagious**.
> Leprosy is endemic in many parts of Africa.
> An epidemic of measles cancelled their plans.

energizing, enervating These similar-looking adjectives are actually opposite in meaning. The first means *giving vitality*, the second *physically weakening, sapping*.
> He ate an energizing breakfast of bacon and eggs with toast.
> Most people find a hot humid climate to be unpleasantly enervating.

English There are three main historical periods, Old English (also called Anglo-Saxon) (800–1100), Middle English (1100–1500), and Modern English (1500–present). The two main dialects of Modern English are American and British. (For further information see DIALECTS, pp. 148–54.)

enormity means *great* but is limited to the context of evil-doing. It is not a synonym for *enormousness* or *hugeness*.
> They never could forgive the enormity of his treachery and deceit.

envisage, envision Both have to do with picturing something in the mind. The first has to do with particular detail; the second may be used to imply something beyond physical reality.
> I had envisaged him happy in his attic studio—before I saw the squalid reality for myself.
> Optimists tend to envision a future free from all pain and strife.

epitome means *representative example*. The verb is **epitomize.**
> In many ways Picasso epitomized the Bohemian artist.

equable, equitable The first means *steady, unchanging, remote from extremes*. The second means *fair, impartial*.

equally as

He had a very equable temper: I never once heard him raise his voice.

Do you think the judge will regard this settlement as equitable?

equally as Do not use in place of either *equally* or *as*.

Doing it quietly is equally important.

(Non-S: Doing it quietly is equally as important.)

We shall be as quiet as mice.

(Non-S: We shall be equally as quiet as mice.)

equitable See **equable**.

et cetera (etc., &c.) is Latin meaning *and so on*. It is used in order to escape having to repeat all the items of a list already given, or as a means of omitting irrelevant material at the end of a quotation. Avoid at all other times: it suggests you don't really know what you're writing about, or else that you can't be bothered to tell the reader.

evangelical, evangelistic The first is strictly limited to a type of Christianity, while the second means *intensely enthusiastic*.

The church next door belonged to an evangelical sect, and we became friends with some of its younger members.

Bill Snow is Australia's most evangelistic anti-tobacco campaigner.

exceptionable, exceptional The first almost always occurs in the negative form **unexceptionable**, meaning *to which no exception may be taken or fault found*. The second is more common and means *unusual*.

Paul's development has generally been unexceptionable, and he shows a remarkable flair for music.

Mozart was obviously an exceptional child.

(in) excess of Hackneyed. Use **more than** instead.

He has more than [not in excess of] five hundred diamonds in that keg.

exorbitant literally means "out of orbit" (no h before orbit), but usually is used in the figurative sense of *excessive, outrageously large*.

expatiate, expostulate The first means *speak or write in detail, develop, expand*, and is followed by **on** or **upon**. The second means *argue persuasively* and should be followed by **about, for, on**, or **upon**.

The preacher expatiated upon the moral of the story, which dealt with the virtues of self-denial.

I had to expostulate at length on the importance of his work before he would agree to withdraw his resignation.

expatriate The misspelling "expatriot" is commonly encountered. (On the other hand, *compatriot* is correct.)

expostulate See **expatiate**.

F

facile means *capable of being done with little effort*, and contains a suggestion of emptiness. It is not generally complimentary.

Your facile argument would not convince a four-year-old.

facility, faculty are sometimes confused in certain contexts. The first means *ease in doing something*, the second *particular ability*. (Avoid using **facility** as a pretentious synonym for hospital, school, or jail.)

Mrs Paston clearly had a facility for writing newsy letters.

He has the faculty of being able to follow four different conversations at once.

factious, factitious, fractious These three words are quite unrelated except by sound. The first has to do with **factions**, or partisan conflicts. The second means *artificial, manufactured, phoney*. The third means *unruly, lacking self-discipline*.

> After the election, the Liberals indulged themselves in an orgy of factious dissent.

> Consumerism is based on the principle that material desires are factitious.

> "Can't you keep that fractious little imp under control?" he asked testily.

factor Often used unnecessarily. Avoid by rewriting.

> The balmy climate was the main factor in their decision to move to Barbados.

> Better: The balmy climate of Barbados was the main reason they moved there.

faculty See **facility**.

farther, further Though the two are often interchanged, some authorities recommend that the first be limited to matters of distance, and the second to quantity or time.

> Heathcliff may be able to swim farther than I, but Emily can swim farthest.

> We were lucky he did not decide to extend his stay further.

faze, phase The first is a colloquial verb meaning *disturb, worry*. Do not confuse it with the noun **phase** which means *aspect* or *stage*.

> He wasn't the least bit fazed by my question.

> Adolescence is perhaps the most difficult phase of our early life.

feasible means *capable of being performed or carried out*. It is not necessarily a synonym for **plausible** or **probable**.

> Would it be feasible to finish the count by tonight?

(Non-S: I don't think it's very feasible that she'll notice the loss.)

feet, foot The following are standard forms:
The arch was sixty feet high.
It was a sixty-foot arch [note hyphen].

fewer, less Use **less** with singular nouns and **fewer** with plural nouns.
We need fewer critics and less dissension if we are to win.

final Use **final** or **latest** instead of **last** to avoid possible ambiguity.
Ambiguous: That's their last offer.
Better: That's their final [alternatively, latest] offer.

finalize Avoid by using **finish, conclude,** or **settle**.

first, firstly First has a wide range of commonly understood meanings. **Firstly** means *in the first place* and should be used only in listing points or topics, as in a debate. **First** can also have this meaning, so **firstly** might well be avoided altogether.

first and foremost Use one or the other, not both.

fix literally means *to make firm, put in an unchanging place*. It is also used in other more colloquial ways, but these may be non-standard. Handle with care.

flammable, inflammable are synonyms meaning *able to be kindled or inflamed*. The traditional form of the word is **inflammable**, but this is now less used because of the fear that children and others may wrongly think it means *non-flammable*, i.e. fireproof. **Inflammable** is still preferred in figurative contexts, however.

flaunt, flout The first means *display openly*, the second *disobey openly*.

> She flaunted her loyalty to the rebels on every possible occasion.

> "How dare you flout your mother's wishes? Leave the room!" he cried.

flounder, founder The first means *thrash about helplessly*, the second *sink to the bottom*.

> They came upon a buck furiously floundering in the middle of a bog.

> By May we realized that the project was in danger of foundering.

folk is like *people* in that it requires a plural verb. "Folks" is non-standard, and should be avoided in formal contexts.

following When used as a synonym for **after**, ambiguity may result.

> Ambiguous: They arrested a young pilot following the fly-past.

> Clearer: They arrested a young pilot after the fly-past had ended.

forbid, prohibit Both have similar meanings, but the first requires the preposition **to**, the second, **from**.

> His mother forbade him to leave the house before morning.

> He was prohibited from leaving until the others had gone.

forced, forceful, forcible The first usually suggests strained action, something unnatural. The second is a more general word, meaning *having to do with force*. The third has to do with brute force or violence.

> At the end of this tiresome joke, Percy gave me a forced smile.

> Faced with such a forceful argument, how could I resist?

> The guards' forcible entry was later discussed in court.

forego, forgo The first means *go before*, *precede*, the second, *do without*.

> The foregoing broadcast was recorded in Amsterdam last winter.

> If you are to lose weight you must forgo your gin and tonic.

forever, for ever The first is acceptable in all situations, though *The Oxford English Dictionary* preserves the distinction between **forever**, meaning *continually*, and **for ever**, meaning *for all time*.

> Mill was forever preaching the gospel of utilitarianism.

> The fame of Florence Nightingale will live for ever.

former and latter should be used only when two things are being discussed. For three or more, use **first** or **foremost** and **last** or **lattermost**.

fortuitous, fortunate The first means *happening by chance*, the second, *having good luck*.

> Their meeting in the frozen food section of the supermarket was entirely fortuitous.

> It was fortunate that you knew she had moved to Chicago.

founder See **flounder**.

fraction is often used to mean *a small part*, though not all fractions are small. Avoid in this sense.

fractious See **factious**.

fulsome, although derived from **full**, is not a complimentary word. It means *excessive*, *cloying*, even *unpalatable*.

> After a time the guide's fulsome praise of the late senator began to irritate my mother.

further See **farther**.

future Often used unnecessarily with words such as **plans** or **prospects**, which themselves convey the notion of futurity.

gambit

You'd better start planning for the future.
Better: You'd better start planning.

G

gambit refers to an opening move that involves some sacrifice. Expressions such as "opening gambit" are redundant.

> The President's gambit at the disarmament talks was to announce the recall of all troops from the Near East.

gender Traditionally a grammatical term only, and not a synonym for sex. Recently feminists have chosen to use the word in the latter sense, however.

> It's curious that the Spanish word *problema* is masculine in gender, while *foto* is feminine.
> Feminist usage: Gender should not determine eligibility for teaching positions.

geriatric means *concerned with the health and welfare of the elderly*. It is not merely a synonym for **senile** or **old person**.

germane, material, relevant All three mean *pertinent to what is being discussed*, but **material** may also mean *necessary, essential*.

> These are irrelevant details, not germane to this discussion.
> He forgot to mention two material points, thereby destroying their argument.

get Do not use **have got** in place of **have** in formal writing. Also note that the preferred form of the participle is **got**, not **gotten**.

> She has no apples.
> (Non-S though common informally: She hasn't got any apples.)

glean means *gather all that remains*. It should not be used to mean *obtain an impression from*.

> She is always gleaning material for her projected biography.
> (Non-S: You can glean some idea of his income from those figures.)

glutton, gourmand, gourmet A glutton cares only for the quantity of food, a gourmet only for its quality. A gourmand is somewhere in between, keenly interested in good food and drink, but inclined to overeat. Only **gourmet** is complimentary.

good, goodly, well The first and second are adjectives with distinct meanings: **good** means *excellent, of high quality* (among many other things); **goodly** means simply *large* and is normally limited to sentences such as "She inherited a goodly fortune." **Well** is the adverbial form of **good**. In informal English **good** is often used as an adverb: this is non-standard in written or formal spoken English. The test for whether you need **good** or **well**: what word in the sentence is most affected by it? If that word is a noun, **good** is required. If it's a verb, **well** is needed. The antonyms of **good**, **well** are **bad**, **badly**, and the same test applies. Here are a few typical idioms using **good** and **well**. Note that there is some divergence between British and American idiom, especially in the use of **bad** and **badly**. For further information see your dictionary.

> You did good [did a good deed]. You did well [performed excellently].
> You look good [seem moral, or are visually attractive].
> You look well [appear in good health].
> I feel bad [Amer. am unhappy or sick, Brit. am inclined to do evil].
> I feel badly [Brit. am unhappy or sick, Amer. have tactile problems].
> I read badly [imperfectly].

gourmand, gourmet See **glutton**.

graffiti

graffiti is a plural Italian noun, meaning *scribblings*, so it must take a plural form of the verb. (A single graffito seems to be as rare as a single spaghetto.)

Spray-painted graffiti are difficult to erase.

gratuitous means *unearned* or *unwarranted*.

I don't care for that sort of gratuitous criticism.

grievous Not "grevious" (in spelling or pronunciation).

grisly, grizzly The first means *horrifying*, *gruesome*, the second *grey*, *grey-haired* (from the French *gris*).

That's one of the most grisly murders I've ever heard of.

The grizzly bear (*Ursus horribilis*) is actually usually brownish.

guerrilla Note spelling. The word is Spanish and refers to someone having to do with war (from Spanish *guerra*, war). Although **guerrilla** is itself quite a neutral term, English-speaking journalists and other news-people have long been conditioned by our governments to link it to supposedly pejorative words such as "Communist" or "anti-government" (as, for example, in El Salvador). By now most Westerners unconsciously react to "guerrilla" as equivalent to enemy. The complimentary and neutral equivalents are "people's freedom-fighter" and "dispossessed peasant"—the latter being what guerrillas usually are. The U.S.-backed contras seeking to overthrow the government of Nicaragua are of course also guerrillas.

guttural Not "gutteral"—think of the guttural speech of the Ural Mountains.

H

hale, hail The first means *healthy, robust* (adj.) or *drag* (verb). The second is a greeting or frozen rain.

> He was so hale and hearty, it took seventeen men to hale him into court.
> "Hail, Caesar!" came the full-throated response.

hangar, hanger The first is where aircraft are kept, the second is a support for hanging clothes.

hanged, hung People in nations which still use this form of execution may be **hanged. Hung** is used in all other contexts. Avoid the expression **hanged to death**, which is redundant.

harangue, tirade The first is a prolonged or tedious speech addressed to at least two people. The second is an abusive speech directed at one or more. They are not synonyms.

hardly Do not use with negative constructions. The correct preposition to follow hardly is **when**, not **than**.

> I could hardly see to the end of the drive.
> (Non-S: I couldn't hardly see to the end of the drive.)
> Hardly had I entered the room when the telephone rang.
> (Non-S: Hardly had I entered the room than the telephone rang.)

hardly X when Y Be sure that X and Y are grammatically identical (e.g., nouns, verbs). The same is true of **no sooner X than** Y.

> I had hardly arrived when he escorted me to our hostess.
> No sooner had I arrived than he escorted me to our hostess.

hare-brained Not "hair-brained"—the allusion is to the rabbit family.

Hebrew

Hebrew is the ancient Semitic language, closely related to Arabic, in which most of the Old Testament books of the Bible were written. It was revived earlier this century as the official language of Israel. Hebrew is not directly related to **Yiddish**, which is German-based, though both languages use the Hebrew alphabet, written from right to left.

help as a verb meaning *prevent oneself* is never followed by **but**.
> She could not help seeing his hat in the corner.
> (Non-S: She could not help but see his hat in the corner.)

historic, historical The first means *something important or memorable*, the second, *something based on past events*.
> Their descendants never forgot that historic date.
> I'm really not a fan of historical novels.

hitherto, previously The first means *until now*, the second *until then*.
> Hitherto we have overlooked petty infractions of this rule.
> By evening the president had made the previously unimaginable decision.

hoard, horde The first describes a secret store of wealth and may also be used as a verb, meaning *amass and stow away precious items*. The second refers to a disorganized and perhaps threatening throng of people.
> The squirrels are hoarding acorns for the winter.
> Hordes of angry shoppers were by now hammering on the doors.

Hobson's choice means no choice at all. Hobson was a British stable-keeper who allowed his customers no say in the horses they were saddled with.

holocaust Often used of World War II, particularly the Nazi destruction of Jewish ghettos. Its literal meaning is *fiery destruction*.

homogenous, homogeneous The first is a technical term, meaning *similar in structure because of common descent*. The second is more commonly used and means *the same in structure, uniform*. Be careful not to confuse the spellings.

That mixture should be pretty homogeneous—you've been
    stirring it for ten minutes at least.

hopefully The standard English meaning is *with hope*. The use of this word to mean *it is hoped that* (usually followed by a comma) may be widespread, but it is still not standard in formal English.

I saw the children waiting hopefully at the gate.
(Non-S but common informally: Hopefully, we'll be back by
    seven.)

horde See **hoard**.

however If its meaning is *nevertheless*, this word must not begin a sentence, and it should be preceded by a semi-colon or comma and followed by a comma. **However** meaning *in whatever way* has no punctuation.

He never said a word, however.
(Non-S: However, he never said a word.)
He said he would come; however, he may not.
However one regards "however", however it should be
    used sparingly.

hung See **hanged**.

I

I, me The first is used as a subject, the second as an object. As a courtesy, one puts **I** and **me** last in any list. If in doubt about whether you need a subject or an object form, try leaving out the other members of the list. Does it still sound right? Avoid the whole business of whether to say "It is I" or "It is me" by rewording your sentence. ("I" is grammatically correct, but "me" conversationally standard.)

Sadie and I went out for a beer. [I went out.]
(Non-S: Me and Sadie went out for a beer. [Me went out?])
The point of the joke was lost on Mother and me. [Lost on me.]
(Non-S: The point of the joke was lost on Jane and I. [Lost on I?])
It was I who said you were wrong.
Better: I said you were wrong.

i.e. stands for the Latin words *id est*, meaning *that is*. Always preceded by a comma, dash, or parenthesis, it may also (but need not) be followed by a comma. The parenthetical phrase which it governs always ends with another comma, dash, or parenthesis. See also **e.g.**

By Independence Day (i.e. the following Sunday) he had finished the march.

if may be used to introduce an actual situation or a hypothetical one. Use an indicative (ordinary) form of the verb if the subject actually exists. Use the subjunctive form if the state is hypothetical or unknown. (See GRAMMAR, p. 17).

If he was tired last night, it was foolish of him to come [indicative—the tiredness presumably existed].
If Blythe were put in charge we would have to get rid of Smythe [subjunctive—the state is still hypothetical].

if and when Use one or the other, not both.

ignorant of Not **ignorant about**.

They remained ignorant of any plan to eliminate the prince.

ilk is a Scots word meaning *of the same family name*. It is often loosely used to mean *of that sort*, but this is non-standard.

ill, sick Ill in British usage usually corresponds to **sick** in

American. **Sick** in British usage refers specifically to symptoms of nausea. See also **nauseated**, **nauseous**. Avoid confusion by using either **nauseated** or **unwell** (or **not well**). (See DIA- LECTS, p. 150, for further distinctions between American and British usage.)

American: He felt sick to (or at) his stomach.
British: He felt sick.
Standard: He felt nauseated.

American: He was sick for three weeks.
British: He was ill for three weeks.
Standard: He was unwell for three weeks.

illusion See **allude**.

immoral See **amoral**.

impact is a noun (the trendy verb "to impact" is non-standard in formal English), and should be used only if you want the idea of something striking another, not as a modish synonym for **impression** or **influence**. The dentists' specialist adjective **impacted** is usually limited to misaligned teeth.

impedance, impediment The first is an electrical term having to do with the resistance of a circuit. The second means *hindrance, defect*.

All his life he suffered from a terrible speech impediment.

impinge is a verb whose literal meaning is *to strike, hit, or touch* (the past participle form of its Latin root gives rise to the noun **impact**); however, it is more frequently used in the figurative sense of *have an effect* or *encroach*. It should be followed by either **on** or **upon**.

The heavy seas were impinging upon the ferry wharf.
The views of Freud have obviously impinged on her mind.
Our campsite must not impinge on the owners' access to the main road.

imply, infer, insinuate

imply, infer, insinuate The first means *suggest*, the second *deduce, work out*. I imply something which you may infer from my implication. **Insinuate** is similar to **imply**, but has bad overtones.

> The evidence implied that his brother had been something of a wastrel.
>
> You are welcome to infer what you like from my words.
>
> "How dare you insinuate such a thing? Get out!" Ida hissed icily.

impracticable, impractical See **practicable, practical**.

in, into Usually the first is used with subjects that are somehow enclosed. The second, **into,** is commonly used with subjects which are in motion. In much colloquial English these distinctions are often blurred.

> He spent that winter in a cottage overlooking a small lake.
>
> The girls dashed into the toy store.
>
> (Non-S but common informally: The girls dashed in the toy store.)

inapt, inept The first means *unsuitable*, the second, *clumsy*.

> A tennis outfit would be inapt to wear to a funeral.
>
> He gave the most inept display of juggling I have ever seen.

(be) inclined to, toward (Amer.), **towards** (Brit.) means *be disposed to*. It is not a synonym for **tend**.

> I'm inclined to believe [or toward(s) believing] Betsy's version of the story.
>
> Summers tend to be hot around here.
>
> (Non-S: Summers are inclined to be hot around here.)

include suggests only part of something larger. See **compose**.

inculcate, inoculate are related in that each has to do with the implanting of something. **Inculcate** means *implant or pass on (ideas)* Note: the ideas are inculcated *in* their recipient. Strictly,

inoculate means *implant* or *inject (serum or vaccine)*, though one may also speak figuratively of inoculating someone's mind with new ideas.

> By the time he was ten his aunt had thoroughly inculcated her vegetarian principles and habits in him.
>
> Have you had an anti-tetanus inoculation recently?

indefinitely means *with infinite limits*. Do not use it as a synonym of "for a very long time"—and note that "almost indefinitely" makes no literal sense at all.

indubitably See **doubtless**.

inductive See **deductive**.

infer See **imply**.

inflammable means *able to be kindled or inflamed*. Recently the word **flammable**, whose meaning is more obvious to all, has begun to replace it in literal contexts, especially on warning labels and signs. **Inflammable** is still preferable in any figurative context.

> That methane mix must be highly flammable; I hope it is well protected.
>
> The situation in Lebanon remains inflammable.

See also **flammable**.

inflict Something is inflicted on someone. Do not confuse with **afflict** (someone with something).

> Job was afflicted with a rash of boils.
>
> God inflicted boils on Job.

ingenious, ingenuous The first means *clever, inventive*, the second *open, innocent*. Note its antonym, **disingenuous**, means *crafty, devious* or *insincere*.

> That was an ingenious solution to the problem. It showed ingenuity.

input

> Our hearts were charmed by her ingenuous air. Her ingenuousness won all.
>
> The captain's disingenuous manner fooled no one.

input An overused vogue word, derived from computer and other electronic specialist vocabulary. Its use as a verb (as in "We must input some ideas") is non-standard except in jocular or colloquial usage. Use "feed in" or something similar.

inside is followed by **of** only when it means *in less than*.

> We left the dog inside the compound [not "inside of"].
>
> They should be back inside of an hour.

insidious, invidious The first means *spreading slowly and stealthily*. The second means *causing ill will, offensive*.

> The insidious virus had finally affected his memory.
>
> The laws against blacks were unjust and invidious.

insightful Not standard. Use **perceptive** instead.

insignia is plural. The singular (which is rarely encountered) is **insigne**.

insinuate See **imply**.

intense, intensive The first refers to something done to a high degree. The second means *concentrated, close*.

> I had never before seen such intense joy shine from a face.
>
> We must make an intensive search of the garage.

interesting To tell someone that what you are about to say is interesting is a good way to ensure they end up feeling it isn't. The same applies to the words **amazing, funny, tragic** and **unusual**. Avoid special pleading: give the relevant details with a minimum of editorial comment. (See STYLE generally, starting on p. 155).

Even more interesting was the fact that the sea had turned
   black.

Better: The sea had turned black, much to their horror.

interface A specialist term (now usually associated with com-
puters) that has worked its way into general usage, having to
do with how components, particularly the surfaces or edges or
circuit boards, are interconnected. Do not use as a synonym
for **interact** or **interaction**.

A good nurse must be able to interact with [deal with,
   handle] newborn babies.

(Non-S: A nurse must be able to interface with neonates.)

interlude, interval The first refers to something presented
between two parts of an entertainment. The second means
space between two given points. Do not use to describe a fixed
period of time.

In the interval between his wife's departure and his mother's
   arrival Carlyle wrote two of his greatest essays.

(Non-S: He'll be away for an interval of eight months.)

After the first act there was a brief orchestral interlude.

in terms of Avoid: usually unnecessary.

What does the posting offer in terms of living accommodation?

Better: What living accommodation does the posting offer?

internment, interment The first means *confinement, imprison-
ment*, the second *burial*.

He suffered fourteen years' internment before the truth
   became known.

The interment will be in Prospect Street Cemetery.

interpretative, interpretive The words are synonyms; either
form is correct.

into

into See **in**.

invidious See **insidious**.

Irish may refer either to the English dialects of Ireland, or to the Celtic language (related to Scots Gaelic) spoken in Ireland.

irony, sarcasm Both occur when the true meaning or outcome of something is the opposite of what is outwardly expressed or expected. Irony may also be used to describe the feigning of ignorance in an argument, though this is more likely to be described as **sarcasm**. Sarcasm has elements of unpleasantness which irony may not. Both irony and sarcasm are difficult concepts to grasp, particularly for children and people just beginning to learn the language. They should be used with the greatest of care, and only where there is no possibility of misunderstanding. The adjectives **ironic** and **ironical** are synonymous.

"Tell me all about it," she sneered sarcastically.

It was ironic(al) that his peace proposals led directly to the worst war the nation had ever known.

irregardless This word is not part of standard English. Use **regardless**. The mistaken form may be the result of the word's similarity to **irrespective**.

its, it's A commonly confused pair. **Its** is the possessive adjective, e.g. its toy. **It's** is the contraction of it is, e.g. it's empty. (See **apostrophe** in TYPOGRAPHY, pp. 132–4.)

-ize Many useful English verbs have been created by adding this suffix to a noun root, e.g., "harmonize" (from "harmony"), "pressurize" (from "pressure"), and "vandalize" (from "vandal"). On the other hand, why create another "-ize" verb if a perfectly good equivalent is already available? Compulsive coiners and users of such words give the impression of being ignorant of the resources of their own language. Handle such creations as "documentize" (write down), "finalize" (finish), "prioritize" (put first), and "summarize" (sum up) with care.

J

jargon See **dialect**.

join together, link together Omit **together**.

K

kind of, sort of, type of There is some disagreement among authorities over the standard forms. The patterns below may be taken as generally acceptable.

What kind of dessert do you like?
(Non-S: What kinds of desserts do you like?)
Those are the kinds of appliance we need.
(Non-S: Those are the kind of appliances we need.)
Do you understand yachts of this sort?
(Non-S: Do you understand these sorts of yachts?)
Ohio River fishermen use six different types of hook [i.e. hook-types].
(Non-S: Ohio River fishermen use six different types of hooks.)

knots means (among other things) *nautical miles per hour*. The expression "knots per hour" is incorrect.

kudos The word is Greek, and means *fame* or *glory*. It requires a singular verb.

"Most of the kudos goes to the director, of course," Armand mused bitterly.

L

languid, limpid The first means *limp, listless*, the second *clear, calm*.

I found Laura lying languidly on a lawn-chair.

The willow was mirrored in the limpid water of the pool.

last, latest may be used as synonyms. **Latest**, however, does not have the connotation of finality that **last** can have, and may need to be used to avoid ambiguity.

The manager asked me to consider the latest offer [the most recent, but not necessarily the last] from Smith Brothers.

He asked me to consider the final offer [the last of a series].

Ambiguous: The manager asked me to consider the last offer.

latter Means *second of two*. See **former**.

laudable, laudatory The first means *deserving praise*, the second *praising*.

Mrs Biskitt made a laudable attempt to play the school song.

The chairman then launched into a long and highly laudatory speech about Dad.

lay, lie The first means *put down, arrange* and is transitive—so it must be followed by a noun or pronoun. Its principal parts are **lay, laid, laid**. The second is an irregular verb, meaning *recline*. Its parts are **lie, lay, lain**. It is not transitive. The two verbs frequently confused in much dialect speech—probably because the past tense of **lie** is **lay**. (Another verb lie, meaning *to tell an untruth*, is regular: its parts are **lie, lied, lied**.)

"Lie down!" he shouted.

(Non-S: "Lay down!" he shouted anxiously at the dog.)

The corpse lay [*or* was lying] on the floor.

(Non-S: The corpse was laying on the floor.)

A mark on the snow showed where he had lain [*or* been lying].

(Non-S: A mark on the snow showed where he had been laying.)

He had laid the pages carefully upon the table.

(Non-S: He had lain the pages carefully upon the table.)

You should lie low for a while.

(Non-S: You should lay low for a while.)

leading question, loaded question These are similar, both being questions designed to bring forth certain answers, as in legal cross-examination. The second is a stronger term, implying some kind of unfairness or treachery on the part of the questioner. See also **question-begging**.

"You'll be good to Jenny, won't you?" is a leading question.

"Have you stopped beating your wife?" is the classic example of a loaded question.

least, less These are the superlative and comparative forms of **little**. Do not use with plural nouns (use **fewer** instead), or as the comparative of **small**. See also **fewer**.

Do you imagine that I am less unhappy than you?

Of all the boys, Barry was the least trouble.

There were fewer people there tonight.

(Non-S: There were less people there tonight.)

Why should you be allowed to pay less [*or* a smaller price]?

(Non-S: Why should you be allowed to pay a less price?)

lectern See **dais**.

less See **least**.

lesser means *not as great as the other(s)*; it is the opposite of **greater**. Do not use as a synonym for *not as big* or *not as large*.

He will be seen by history as one of our lesser leaders.

(Non-S: Would you be willing to accept a lesser sum for your painting? (Use "smaller" instead.))

level, mark In standard English usage, there must be a physically visible level or mark when either of these words is used.

Last week interest rates dropped below twelve per cent.

(Non-S: Last week interests dropped below the twelve per cent level.)

The mercury passed the forty-degree mark an hour ago.

liable to See **apt to**.

licence, license In British usage the first is the noun, and the second is the verb, corresponding to similar standard English pairs such as **advice, advise** and **prophecy, prophesy**. But in American usage **license** is both noun and verb, and "licence" is non-standard. (See DIALECTS, pp. 151–2.)

lighted, lit Both are standard past tense forms of the verb **light**. The first is more commonly used as an adjective.

He lit the seven-branched candelabra with reverential care.

Don't bring that lighted match anywhere near the tank.

lie meaning *recline* has the principal parts **lie, lay, lain**. See **lay**.

light-years refer to distance, not time. One light-year is the distance that light travels in a year, i.e. approximately 6,000,000,000,000 miles.

like meaning *similar to (but not including)* must not be used to modify a verb—**as** or **if** should be used instead. In formal English, **such as** is required if the meaning is *similar to (and including)*. Like should not be used as a substitute for the conjunction **as**.

I have never seen so many men that looked like utter wastrels.

For wines such as those, you need a proper cellar.

Play it as you played it last night.

(Non-S: Play it like you did last night.)

It seemed as if he was feeling unwell.

(Non-S: It seemed like he was feeling unwell.)

likely meaning *probably* is usually preceded by **more, most** or **very**. See also **apt to**.

He'll very likely be back before sunset. He was more likely to do it.

limited should, in formal English, be used only in a literal or concrete sense.

Of course, we have a limited amount of money for this project.

(Non-S: We can expect only limited help from her friends.)

limpid See **languid**.

lingua franca A language used for communication within and between nations which speak different languages. Standard English is the leading lingua franca of our time. See **dialect**.

linguist has two distinctive meanings: *student of linguistics* and *speaker of two or more languages*. Avoid confusion by using **polyglot** or a qualification such as **bilingual** if you intend the latter meaning.

My aunt's Asian travels have made her into something of a polyglot.

link together Omit **together**.

lion's share has connotations of selfishness or greediness. Do not use if these are not part of what you wish to communicate.

(Non-S: The lion's share of the estate went to her devoted companion.)

lit See **lighted**.

literally Do not use this other than of something which is actually true.

livid, lurid

I almost died of fright.

(Non-S: I literally died of fright.)

He literally died of fright: the unexpected apparition brought about a fatal stroke.

livid, lurid The first has two meanings: *bluish-grey* and *furious*. The second means *glowing through haze* or *harsh, shocking*. Do not mistakenly use either as a synonym for **vivid**, meaning *bright, striking*.

The livid tones of the northern winter dominate her paintings.

The lurid details of the murder were the talk of the town.

loan The standard verb means *make a financial loan to*. Do not use as a vague synonym for **lend**.

The bank loaned him what he needed to have the foundations poured.

(Non-S but common informally: Would you loan me some of those old *Life* magazines?)

local residents The first word may usually be omitted.

locate as a formal verb means *put in place, establish*. In careful usage it is not an exact synonym for **situate**, which has to do with the site of a physical object such as a building. In informal English **locate** is often used as a synonym for **find**.

The directors located their new offices in the Regal Building.

The parking plaza is situated on the south side of the square.

(Non-S but common colloquially: "I just can't locate my spectacles," quavered Grandpa.)

loose, lose The first is the adjective, the second the verb. The two are frequently confused.

The lion was running loose in the streets.

How could you lose an elephant?

lots meaning *much* or *many* is informal only. **A lot of**, meaning the same thing, is acceptable except in the most formal contexts.

lunch, luncheon The second has overtones of grandeur, so should be reserved for suitable occasions.

lurid See **livid**.

luxuriant, luxurious The first means *growing thickly*; the second is the adjectival form of the noun **luxury**.
  The luxuriant lawn was too much for the mower.
  I had grown tired of our luxurious life.

M

majority, minority Each of these implies the existence of the other. Use only in speaking of things that can be counted. Avoid the cliché "the vast majority" by using **most** instead.
  A minority of the staff members are refusing to take part at all.
  (Non-S: I do the majority of my shopping on Tuesday.)

marginal means *on the edge of*, *near the lower limit of*. Do not use as a synonym for **slight** or **small**.
  Most illiterates know only a marginal standard of living.
  (Non-S but common informally: There has been a marginal improvement in his condition.)

mark See **level**.

masterful, masterly The first means *commanding, domineering*, the second, *skilled, highly proficient*. The adverb for both is **masterfully**.
  Phinney's wife finally rebelled against his masterful ways.

material

> Masterly performances of Bach's Trio Sonatas for organ are rare indeed.

material See **germane**.

materialize meaning *develop, happen, occur* is usually better replaced by another word. A common slip is unwittingly to apply it to the wrong noun in a sentence, as in the Non-S example below.

> Bad weather did not develop, in spite of earlier threats.
>
> (Non-S: Earlier threats of bad weather did not materialize.)

maximize, minimize These terms have to do with size, the first meaning *make as large as possible*, and the second *make as small as possible*. Their use should be limited to literal contexts.

> Careful sales campaigns should enable us to maximize profits.
>
> (Non-S: The president attempted unsuccessfully to minimize the bad news. ["Play down" would be more suitable.])

may See **can**.

me See **I/me**.

mean See **average**.

meaningful An overworked adjective. Present what is meaningful and let others derive their own conclusions.

means meaning *money* always requires a plural verb-form. When it means *way of achieving something* it may be taken as being either singular or plural.

> The means available are not enough for you to live on until December.
>
> The end result may have seemed enlightened, but the means needed to reach it was [singular] unethical.

"There are [plural] other means of getting the job done,"
said Smee warningly.

media is the plural of **medium**, meaning *agency, means of communication*. In standard English it is followed by a plural verb,
though informal use of **media** with singular verbs is extremely
common.

By Thursday the media were [plural] giving full details of
the robbery.

(Non-S but common in informal use: "The media, my dear,
is [singular] becoming tiresome.")

median See **average**.

mediate See **arbitrate**.

memento Often incorrectly spelled "momento"—remember
re*mem*ber.

metal, mettle The first refers to metallic elements such as iron,
copper, and gold. The second means *courage, spirit*.

Look for the vertical metal strip near the right edge of the
door.

The Swedes' challenge should test France's mettle, if anything does.

meticulous means *fussy, overcareful, overthorough*. It is not complimentary. Use **careful, painstaking** or **scrupulous** if you
intend no slight.

Pontifax's meticulous accounting procedures finally drove
us mad.

mettle See **metal**.

Middle English See **English**.

militate against, (be) mitigated by

militate against, (be) mitigated by The first means *counteract strongly*. The second means *be assuaged, lessened, moderated by*.

>We mustn't do anything that might militate against our chances.

>The horror of the deed was somewhat mitigated by the kindness the criminal had shown to his victims afterwards.

millennium means *thousand years*. The plural is either **millennia** or **millenniums**. This is a word which will undoubtedly be used more frequently as we approach the year 2000, so get the spelling right—two ls and two ns.

minimize See **maximize**.

minuscule Often misspelled (and mispronounced) "miniscule"—think of something so small it is almost a **minus** quantity.

minute detail The first word of this cliché is usually unnecessary.

mitigate See **militate**.

Modern English See **English**.

modus vivendi is Latin meaning *way of life*. The term is used to denote a truce between combatants, an agreement they can live with until a final settlement has been reached. As with all Latinisms, it should not be used unless you wish to give your writing a scholarly or pedantic air.

>The uneasy modus vivendi continued for less than five weeks.

moment, momentum The first means *importance*, the second *impetus, onward movement*.

>We all agreed that a visit from Mr Squires would be a matter of great moment.

The momentum of the runaway tram carried it halfway up the other side of the valley.

more than one is followed by a singular verb.
More than one sailor has [singular] at times wished he had stayed ashore.

moribund means *death-bound, on the point of death*. It is often mistakenly used as a synonym for **dormant**, **struggling** or **troubled**.
The slide-rule industry is now moribund as a result of the introduction of cheap pocket calculators.

motivate means *cause to act a certain way*. It does not mean *supply a motive, justify*.
His evident fear motivated me to call upon the doctor that evening.
(Non-S: You don't have to motivate your actions to me, you know.)

mutual means *shared between two*. See also **common**.
Jenkins and I discovered we had a mutual friend in Andover.
The mutual love of the twins was what kept them isolated.

myself is used correctly as a reflexive pronoun or for emphasis. Do not use it, however, as a means of avoiding **I** or **me**. See also **I, me**.
I washed myself. I had to wax the floor myself.
(Non-S: John and myself walked into town [should be "I"].)
(Non-S: He gave the title to my wife and myself [should be "me"].)

N

nadir, zenith The first means *lowest point*. It is often mistakenly used as though it were a synonym of **zenith**, which means *highest point*. They are actually antonyms.

nation refers to the political and social aspects of a place. See **country**.

nature Avoid vague expressions which use **nature** as a vague synonym for **quality**. Even in particular applications having to do with the outdoors and the primeval state of things, **nature** and **natural** are overused. Be more explicit.

> We were soon to encounter a crime of a most perplexing nature.
> Better: We were soon to encounter a most perplexing crime.
> He was a true lover of nature.
> Better: He loved outdoor sports, particularly hiking, skiing, and swimming.

nauseated, nauseous The first means *feeling queasy*, the second, *causing feelings of queasiness*.

> The movement of the coach had made me feel quite nauseated.
> She had painted the kitchen a nauseous puce.

need meaning *require* should be followed either by a gerund (a noun made out of a verb + **-ing**) or an object and a past participle, or an infinitive. (See GRAMMAR, p. 15 for more on gerunds and participles.)

> This floor needs washing.   I need this floor washed.
> I need to go.

neither X nor Y means *not X and not Y either*. Its positive equivalent is **either X or Y**. In both cases, the verb should agree with the noun nearest it. When **neither** is used on its own, the verb is always singular. Do not use **neither** as a means of intensifying a negative.

> Neither gold nor silver is [singular] to be found anywhere in the land.
>
> Neither the president nor his personal troops were [plural] to survive the night.
>
> Neither of the gurus seems [singular] to know much about yoga, Lazlo thought.
>
> (Non-S: "You're not coming, neither," Blanche hurled defiantly.)

nemesis comes from the name of the Greek goddess of deserved punishment or retribution. Do not use as a vague synonym for long-standing enmity or rivalry.

> He met his nemesis when, after one too many binges, he drove his car off a sixty-foot cliff.

new Often unnecessary, as when preceding such words as *breakthrough*, *development*, *discovery* and *finding*.

nice Possibly the vaguest and most overworked adjective in English. The meanings *precise, subtle* are standard; for other meanings such as *pretty, beautiful* and *pleasant* use more precise words. Your thesaurus will provide many suggestions.

> A nice distinction may be made between growing older and growing up.

no Either start with a capital letter and treat as a quote, or do neither.

> After some thought he said he would have to answer no.
>
> "No, I refuse to dance for them," Anitra answered.

nobody is regarded as a singular noun. The singular possessive **his** is conventionally used with it to cover both sexes. Nevertheless, if you're sensitive to the politics of linguistic sexism, you may decide to use a plural noun (e.g., **people**) instead, thus avoiding the whole problem. See GRAMMAR, for agreement in number (p. 21).

> Nobody is forced to sign away his property to the government.
>
> People are not forced to sign away their property to the government.

noisome, noisy The first means *annoying, objectionable, offensive*. The second means *having to do with noise*.

> "Why don't you stop this noisome charade?" she pleaded.
>
> The noisy crowd became silent.

none Use either a singular or a plural verb, but do not change from one to the other in the same sentence.

> None is so lacking in self-confidence as the worker just out of work.
>
> None of the Cambridge group are coming to Becky's party.
>
> (Non-S: None of us has to stay there any longer today, and none are expected to go tomorrow either.)

non sequitur is Latin for *something which does not logically follow*. It is used as a noun in standard English.

> His paper on the physiology of suicide in lemmings was flawed by several non sequiturs, I thought.

no question but, of, that See **question**.

nor Use only when preceded by **neither**. See **neither**.

> She is neither pretty nor rich, but she is kind-hearted.

normalcy, normality. The first is newer and mainly American-based, the second is the traditional standard form. Both mean *state of being normal*.

not all Note the distinction between these two sentences.

> Not all is well in the kingdom [some things are not well].
>
> All is not well in the kingdom [everything is not well].

not only X but Y Be sure to place the **not only** and the **but** (which may also be linked with **also, as well,** or **too**) immediately before the Xs and Ys they qualify. The Xs and Ys must be grammatically similar, e.g. both adjectives, nouns, and so forth. See also **only**.

He was not only as mean as a bear but as fast as a snake as well.

not so much X as Y A common mistake is to use **but** instead of **as** at the end of this construction.

He was not so much a teacher as a firm friend for many years.

(Non-S: He was not so much a teacher but a firm friend for many years.)

no way The standard meaning is *no path or passage.* The meaning *absolutely not* is informal only. **There is no way that . . .** is informally used to mean *it is out of the question that . . . .*

Try as he might he could find no way out of the labyrinth.

(Non-S but common informally: "And as for bringing the dog along—no way!" Father added.)

(Non-S but common informally: "There's no way I'm going to climb up there alone," Roy muttered.)

number of When preceded by **the** use a singular verb-form; when preceded by **a,** use a plural.

The number of absentees this term is [singular] positively amazing.

A number of books were [plural] damaged by a leak in the library roof.

O

O, oh Both are interjections. The first is always spelled with a capital letter, and is always followed by the name of someone (or something) being addressed. It is never followed by a punctuation mark. The second, by contrast, stands alone, indicating surprise, disgust, melancholy, and other overwhelming emotions; it may also be used to signal a pause or break in a spoken sentence. It is always followed either by a comma or an exclamation mark.

"My heart is yours, O April," writes the poet.

"Oh! What was that?" cried Aunt Polly.

He moved to the valley, oh, about twenty years ago.

obligate, oblige are synonyms. The first is American-based, perhaps derived from the Spanish-American *obligado*. (In Britain **obligate** is a legal term.) The second is the standard English form throughout the world.

"I feel obliged to repay your kindness somehow," Maude murmured.

oblivious means *unaware, unconscious*, and may be followed by either **of** or **to**. In writing, the word is generally used by someone observing someone else.

The couple seemed oblivious of the rocks against which their marriage was about to be dashed.

She remained oblivious to her brother's pleas for help.

obsolete, obsolescent The first means *out-of-date*, the second, *becoming obsolete*.

The mechanical calculator is obsolete.

By the mid-80s compact discs had made vinyl records obsolescent.

obviate means *make unnecessary*, not *reduce*.

The new booking system will obviate customers' having to make advance reservations.

(Non-S: Insulation will greatly obviate the effect of the chill winter winds.)

occur usually refers to something unscheduled or accidental. Use **take place** for planned events.

> The wedding will take place at her maternal grandparents' mansion.

> While he was standing there, something quite bizarre occurred.

oculist, ophthalmologist, optician, optometrist Eye specialists love the look of long words, one sees. The first two terms refer to medical practitioners who specialize in eye diseases. An **optician** fills prescriptions for corrective lenses; an **optometrist** tests eyes and prescribes whatever lenses may be needed.

off when used as a preposition is not followed by *of*.

> Please get your car off my driveway.

> (Non-S: "Get your feet off of the tablecloth, you big lug," she screamed.)

Old English See **English**.

on, upon as prepositions denoting physical location are interchangeable. Use whichever you prefer.

> Put the lid upon the pot, then set the tureen on the table.

one (you) may be used as a pronoun, in place of **I**, especially in contexts of habitual or generalized action. Be sure to use **one** (object form), **one's** (possessive form), and **oneself** (reflexive form) along with it. Overuse of **one** tends to sound stilted and even more offensive than overuse of **I**; and may be an indication that the habitual focus of your attention needs changing. In informal English, **you** is often used as an acceptable substitute. **One, I,** and **you** used in this way usually imply an opposing **they**, constituted of people in some way unlike the speaker.

> One shouldn't have to give all one's money to the poor, leaving one with nothing for oneself. Even they would agree, I'm sure.

one of the most

    Informal: I realize you can't believe everything you see on
    TV.

one of the most [adjective] [plural noun] An overused formula, especially when the adjective is a word such as beautiful,
comic, dramatic, exciting, tragic or wonderful. Avoid special
pleading; try to make the facts themselves convey the desired
effect.

one of the, one of those are both followed by plural verbs.
    He is one of the fastest men that plan to run tomorrow.
    She was one of those overbearing matrons that frequent
       Sardi's at four.

one or more is followed by a plural verb.
    One or more of them have to pass the test, or I lose my job.

ongoing is a modish adjective meaning *continuing*. Its associ-
ation with US State Department propaganda during the Viet-
nam War has given it a certain taint. Better avoided.

only The rules governing **only** are many and complex. The
safe thing to do is put it as close as you can to the word you
want to limit. Try to rephrase your meaning if ambiguity or
clumsiness persists. The examples below show the most
common patterns.
    He only watered five plants yesterday [did nothing else to
       them].
    He watered only five plants [not more than five].
    Only he was a child [the others were older].
    He was only a child [not older].
    He was a child only [nothing more].
    He was an only child [no other].
    He only tries to please [with spoken emphasis on
       tries=doesn't really want to please].
    He only tries to please [with spoken emphasis on please =
       doesn't intend anything other than pleasing].

In speaking sentences with **only** we usually emphasize certain other words in order to underline our meaning. What is quite clear in speech may turn out to be quite ambiguous in written form, as the last two examples show. Be aware of this possibility; it may be necessary to rewrite the sentence.

opposite See **contrary**.

optimum means *best*. It usually connotes some degree of compromise between opposing tendencies.

> As soon as the generator had reached its optimum speed (i.e. not too fast and not too slow), the boss threw the switch.

or between listed items implies each is considered separately. A singular verb is called for.

> Smoked salmon or Caerphilly cheese is all we have to offer, I'm afraid.

oral, verbal The first means *of the mouth*, the second, *of words*. Use **oral** to describe spoken, as opposed to written, English. **Verbal** is useful mainly as a contrast to *non-verbal*, i.e. having to do with symbols, body language, music and other meaningful manifestations around us.

> As so far they had only an oral agreement, I suggested that they first draw up and sign a contract.
> The genius of Graves's poetry is not to be found merely in its verbal content.
> Semiotics is the study of non-verbal communication.

orient, orientate meaning *point in a specific direction* are synonyms. Both tend to be overused: use something simpler or be more specific, or both.

> It was a technology-oriented school where the arts were depreciated.
> Better: The school emphasized technology; the arts were depreciated.

other than

other than may be used where **other** is an adjective or noun. Do not use **other than** as an adverb; use **otherwise than** or **other than as being**.

> "I want to go somewhere other than Bianchi's," the producer said.

> She wished he would regard her otherwise than as a mother.

> She wished he would regard her other than as being a mother.

> (Non-S: She wished he would regard her other than as a mother.)

out of is the standard prepositional form. The dialect **out** on its own is often heard.

> Gary hurled the flaming object out of the room, then flattened himself on the floor.

> (Non-S: "He actually threw the cat out the window," Gertrude gasped.)

outside when used as an adverb is not followed by a preposition. The expression "outside of" is standard only when **outside** is used as a noun, as in speaking of the outside of a house.

> Montreal is the largest French-speaking city outside France.

> (Non-S but common informally: "Leave your boots outside of the door," he called.)

outstanding may mean either *distinguished* (as in "outstanding scholar") or *overdue* (as in "outstanding account"). Do not use if any ambiguity is likely to result.

over, overly are adverbs. The first is the standard form. The second is a common American alternative.

> Try not to appear over-anxious.

> American: Try not to appear overly anxious.

owing to is equivalent to **because of**. See also **due to**.

He asked the children to walk up from the corner, owing to
   his lateness.

P

pace X is a form of the Latin for *with peace to X* (where X =
someone's name) but in academic and scholarly circles it is
taken to mean *in spite of what X says*. Use only if you feel you
must.
   The island was, *pace* Guillemot, considerably less than four
      leagues in length.
   Better: In spite of what Guillemot had reported, the island
      was much less than four leagues long.

panacea means *universal cure for all ailments*.
   The huckster, who had claimed that his elixir was a true
      panacea, was tarred and feathered and run out of town.

parameter, perimeter The first is a technical word from the
areas of crystallography, topography, and higher mathematics. (See your dictionary for further details.) The second
means *outer limit*. Many educated people use **parameter** at
times when **perimeter** or **limit** would be more suitable.
   He explained the responsibilities of company directors.
   (Non-S jargon: He outlined the parameters of the directorial
      level of corporate management.)

partially, partly are generally interchangeable. **Partially** is
often reserved for the meaning *to a certain degree*, and **partly**
for the idea of a part of something rather than the whole thing.
   What he said was partially true: the table was partly in the
      shade.

parody, pastiche The first means *funny or grotesque imitation*;

the second, *artistic work made up of bits from various sources* or *hodgepodge*.

> "Omeletto" turned out to be an operatic parody of *Hamlet*.
> Stravinsky's *Pulcinella* is a pastiche of tunes from the works of an earlier composer, Pergolesi.

past Redundant when followed by words such as **achievements**, **experience**, **history** and **precedents**, all of which already imply the past.

> Let us not dwell only on our achievements.
> (Non-S: Let us not dwell only on our past achievements.)

patois See **dialect**.

peaceable, peaceful The first means *not quarrelsome or hostile*, the second, *quiet, tranquil*.

> In spite of their competitive and stressful jobs, they seem a peaceable group.
> He rode past the valley of the flood, now peaceful in the September sun.

pedagogue, pedant The latter refers to someone who ostentatiously displays book learning or who is over-fussy about grammar, spelling, and the other aspects of usage that are the concern of this book. Until recently **pedagogue** was an accepted synonym for **teacher**, but for many today it has the same uncomplimentary overtones as does **pedant**.

people, public The [national adjective] **people and the** [national adjective] **public** have similar meanings. The first is commonly linked with political support or opposition, the second with cultural and corporate activity. Check your dictionary for further meanings. While **people** always takes a plural verb-form, **public** may be either singular or plural.

> The Canadian people will make their choice at the polls.
> The New Zealand public has a right to know the truth [the public in general].

The American public are obviously inconvenienced by the present highway speed limits [individual members of the population].

percentage Do not use unless the idea of a numerical figure is inherent in the facts conveyed. See also **portion** and **proportion**.

We discussed what percentage of our net income should be used to finance off-shore petroleum exploration.

(Non-S: You will have to do a certain percentage of the cleaning.)

perpetrate, perpetuate The first means *commit, perform*; the second, *make perpetual, prolong*.

The police soon caught the villain who had perpetrated the theft.

The Franconians seemed bent on perpetuating the war.

perquisite, prerequisite The first means *casual profit, incidental benefit*. The second means *something needed before something else*.

A perquisite of being an airline employee is that you may fly anywhere you like for a tenth of the normal fare.

A prerequisite for going on a canoe trip is getting a canoe.

persistence, persistency are synonyms meaning *steadfastly continuing in one's course*. The first has the additional meaning of *survival*.

The persistence [not persistency] of crash victims in below-freezing temperatures has astounded scientists.

He was rewarded for his persistency [or persistence] by a glimpse of the enemy.

personally Avoid using as a means of dressing up a first-person opinion; it only makes the speaker or writer appear insecure.

I personally feel that we must bite the bullet; there is no alternative.

perspicacious, perspicuous

Better: We must bite the bullet; there is no alternative.

perspicacious, perspicuous The first means *insightful*; the second, *clearly expressed, easily comprehended*. The nouns are **perspicacity** and **perspicuity**.

It was most perspicacious of the butler to have noticed the state of Miss Thistle's riding boots.

Although this poem contains no striking new insight, it is pleasantly perspicuous.

persuade See **convince**.

persuasion, suasion are synonyms meaning *winning over, convincing*. The second is more bookish, and is usually limited to general and abstract terms such as **moral suasion**.

peruse means *study carefully*. It is not a synonym for *read quickly* or *skim*.

Uncle Henry perused her sonnet for a full ten minutes.

phenomena is plural. **Phenomenon** is its singular.

Bunker claims that all so-called extra-sensory phenomena have rational explanations.

A triple rainbow is an extremely unusual phenomenon.

Philippines Note spelling. A native is a **Filipino**.

plaid, tartan Both are of Scottish origin. The first means *shawl-like garment*; the second refers to cloth with a clan's distinctive patterning, or to the distinctive patterning itself.

Morag threw her plaid over her shoulders and stepped outside.

"Weave me six ells of tartan," the crone cried. "Mackenzie tartan, mind!"

plan ahead A tautology. Omit **ahead**.

pleonasm, redundancy, solecism, tautology The first two and the last convey the general idea of using more words than are strictly necessary. **Solecism**, meaning *any violation of grammar or idiom*, includes the others.

plethora means *excessive number*. It is not merely a synonym for **much** or **many**.

> Without doubt there has been a plethora of parties this summer.

plus in standard English is a preposition meaning *with the arithmetical addition of*. It normally accompanies a singular verb. Informally, **plus** is commonly used as being equivalent to the conjunction **and**, which requires a plural verb. This is not standard, however.

> The balance plus the surplus represents [singular] our net annual income.
>
> (Non-S but common informally: The holiday plan plus the retirement scheme are irresistible [Standard: replace "plus" with "and"].)

podium See **dais**.

pore over, pour The first means *examine or consider carefully*, the second refers to a flow of liquid.

> She pored over the problem while he poured himself a port.

portentous, pretentious The first has three meanings, *ominous*, *prodigious* and *pompous*. The second means *affecting grandeur or importance*, *showy*.

> The leaden skies seemed a portentous warning to the raftsmen.
>
> Peterson shows a portentous capacity for fast fingerwork.
>
> Mrs Vankleek had a faintly portentous manner of making announcements which was not in itself unattractive.
>
> Many Romans were repelled by such pretentious ceremony.

portion, proportion Both have to do with dividing something. The first means *share*; it is often used informally to mean *part*, but this should be avoided in formal writing. The second means *comparative share* or *part*, and implies some sort of numerical ratio. See also **percentage**.

His portion of pudding was undoubtedly larger than mine.

(Non-S but common informally: The lower portions of the St Francis River are prone to annual flooding.)

His legs seemed short in proportion to the rest of his body.

possible implies uncertainty, so verbs which also imply this, such as **may**, are redundant. Omit **possible** or change the verb.

It's possible that he will come to dinner. He may come to dinner.

(Non-S: It's possible that he may come to dinner.)

practicable, practical A commonly confused pair. The first means *able to be put into practice or use*. The second means *showing common sense or experience* (though a **practical joke** shows neither of these, being merely some sort of physical jest, usually causing discomfort or embarrassment to someone else).

Edison had first to find a practicable way to make a long-lived electric light filament.

The story tells us that the practical pig built his house of bricks.

His idea of a practical joke was to put a tack on a chair.

practically, virtually The first means *in practice* or *to all practical purposes*. Do not use in standard English unless this is true. The second, meaning *almost*, may be used more loosely.

By Friday the celebrations were practically over, although they had been advertised as continuing until Sunday.

The box of chocolates I had left on the table was now virtually empty, with only five or six of the less desirable sorts remaining.

practice, practise The second is not part of American usage, in which **practice** does duty as both noun and verb. In British English, as with standard pairs such as **advice, advise** and **prophecy, prophesy**, the c-spelling denotes the noun and the s-spelling the verb. (See DIALECTS, p. 151–2.)

precipitant, precipitate, precipitous The first two are figurative and roughly synonymous, but the first has connotative meanings of *sudden, hasty,* and the second *rash, unthinking*. The third means *steep, like a precipice*. Avoid the cliché "precipitous decline" by using "sudden drop" instead.

> Winston's entry coincided with the precipitant departure of at least a half-dozen mice and a couple of fat grey rats.
> Precipitate words will only make your fellow-workers nervous.
> The horses steadily inched their way down the precipitous track.

pre-empt means *obtain for oneself in advance* (think of someone emptying the box of goodies before you get there). It is not a synonym for **prevent**.

> Later he found that title to the property had already been pre-empted by his uncle.

prefer is followed by **to**, except when the preference is expressed as an infinitive, when **rather than** should be used.

> "I prefer dancing to sitting," Jonas answered defensively.
> "I prefer to do things rather than to talk about them," Jane retorted.

preferable to means *more desirable than*, so it must not be preceded by **more**.

> Your plan seems much (far, greatly, or vastly) preferable to Johnson's.
> (Non-S: He thought leaving the dog there would be more preferable.)

preference for X over Y, X in preference to Y

preference for X over Y, X in preference to Y are the standard forms.

I have a preference for spending money over saving it.

I tend to spend money in preference to saving it.

prejudice may refer to either bias or detriment, though in both there is a sense of some kind of decision made in advance of the facts. In the first meaning, it is usually followed by **against**; in the second, by **to**.

He admitted that he was already prejudiced against the defendant.

He clearly intended this letter to be without prejudice to any legal action that might arise later.

premises meaning *place of business* has no singular form, and always takes a plural verb.

His Flood Street premises were destroyed by fire.

prerequisite See **perquisite**.

prescribe, proscribe The first means *dictate, lay down as a rule*, the second *prohibit*.

He prescribed that no outbuilding should be visible from the house.

Until recent times, usury was absolutely proscribed; now it is tolerated throughout the world.

presently may mean either *at once* or *in a short while*. Avoid possible misunderstanding by using another word.

Ambiguous: The minister announced that he would retire presently.

prestigious has an archaic meaning, *magical, delusive* (as in conjuring tricks and juggling, often jocularly called "prestigitation"), and a general (and much more common) one, *having prestige, worthy of esteem*.

Houdini's escapes and prestigious feats soon made him famous.

She had never dreamed of winning such a prestigious prize.

presumptive, presumptuous The first means *based on presumption*, and is most commonly used as a legal term. The second means *presuming too much, over-bold, impudent.*

The Prince of Wales is the heir apparent and his son Prince William the heir presumptive to the British throne.

The lawyer's face flushed with anger as the presumptuous speech ended.

pretentious See **portentous**.

prevaricate, procrastinate The first means *be evasive*, the second, *put off till tomorrow.*

He tried to be honest at all times, but now he found himself prevaricating in order to shield his son.

Procrastination is the best way to make the most of time, as long as you make sure never to miss a deadline.

prevent when followed by a participle takes the preposition **from**. If it is followed by a gerund, no preposition is used.

You can't prevent me from going [participle].

You can't prevent my going [gerund].

(Non-S but common informally: "You can't prevent me going," Irene argued.)

preventative, preventive are interchangeable synonyms meaning *that which prevents something from happening*. The second, being shorter, may be preferable.

principal, principle An oft-confused pair. The first is an adjective meaning *main, most important*; it also may do duty as a noun, as in **school principal** (who is always your pal, of course). The second means *fundamental belief, theory, or truth.*

prior to

> My principal objection to old houses is that they are expensive to maintain.

> The lecture was on the principles of the internal combustion engine.

prior to Use **before** instead.

pristine means *original*, *mint*, *unspoiled*, though it is commonly used as a vague synonym for **clean** or **spotless**.

> They planned to restore the steam engine to pristine condition.

procrastinate See **prevaricate**.

prodigal means *wasteful*.

> You'll regret being so prodigal of your fuel supply when winter really sets in.

prognosis refers to prediction of the outcome of a disease or problem. See also **diagnosis**.

> The doctor's prognosis was that the fever would break that night.

prohibit See **forbid**.

prone, prostrate, recumbent, supine All have to do with lying down. The easiest to remember is **supine**, which is lying on the back (think of "spine"). **Prone** and **prostrate** refer to lying face downwards. **Recumbent** is lying in any comfortable position.

prone to refers to habitual unpleasant occurrences. See **apt to**.

> His old dog was prone to sudden blackouts and fainting spells.

prophecy, prophesy The first is the noun, the second the verb. (See DIALECTS, pp. 151–2.)

The count's prophecy came true; in fact, everything he had prophesied took place within three days.

(in) proportion to Do not use unless some kind of numerical ratio is intended. See also **percentage** and **portion**.

The head of the figure she had drawn did not seem in proportion to the rest of the body.

proscribe See **prescribe**.

prostrate See **prone**.

protagonist, proponent The first means *single leading character in a drama or story*; the second, *advocate, champion*.

In the second act the protagonist finds there is still hope.

Mr Forrest is a well-known proponent of silviculture.

protest means *affirm solemnly*. As a standard English verb it is commonly followed by **against** or (less commonly) **in favour of**. In American usage, **against** is commonly omitted.

Lachlan protested his innocence with all the sincerity he could muster.

They plan to protest against the announced price-hikes.

(American: They plan to protest the price-hikes.)

proved, proven Both are past participles of the verb **prove**. The second usage is mainly American, though **proven** is the standard adjectival form everywhere.

I thought he had proved (Amer. proven) that at the outset, but I was mistaken.

Lightbottom, a jockey of proven ability, is expected to win.

provided, providing meaning *if* are interchangeable. Both sound long-winded.

I'll go provided [or providing] I can take the dog.

Better: I'll go if I can take the dog.

prudent, prudential The first means *showing care, foresight*; the second, *about prudence*.

It seemed prudent of Melissa to bar the door that night.

Father presented me with a number of prudential suggestions.

pry has two distinct meanings, *inquire nosily*, and *force (apart)*. (British also uses **prise** for the second meaning.)

Miss Perry, who had obviously been prying, never returned to our house.

In a few moments they had pried [Brit. prised] open the crate.

purport means *give the appearance or idea of*. It should not be used passively (see GRAMMAR, p. 14, for an explanation of passive verb forms), or of people.

The writing purports to be that of Mozart himself.

(Non-S: The writing is purported to be that of Mozart himself.)

These letters purport that you are aware of the problem.

(Non-S: Your accountant purports that you are aware of the problem.)

purposefully, purposely The first means *with an objective in mind*; its antonym is **purposeless**. The second means *deliberately, intentionally*.

I noticed him later walking purposefully towards the telephone.

I believe you purposely upset the tray to cause a diversion.

pyrrhic victory refers to a battle whose cost was too high even for the winners. It is not a synonym for **hollow triumph**.

In the end, the government may discover today's vote to have been a pyrrhic victory.

Q

quandary Note spelling: the word is not "quandry"—even though it usually sounds that way.

quantum is a term from physics, and means *showing a discernible advance from one plane to another*. It is often used informally as a vague synonym for "large"—particularly in the cliché **quantum leap**. Avoid in formal contexts.

question-begging means *arguing in a circle*. See also **leading question, loaded question**.
> Question-begging: How do I know he is a man of taste? Because he smokes El Choko cigars. All men of taste smoke El Choko.

(no) question but, of, that The usual meanings: (1) *certainly* (chiefly dialect and informal), which is followed by an independent clause, (2) *no possibility of*, which is followed by a noun or other substantive, and (3) *no doubt that* (the formal equivalent of 1), also followed by an independent clause. (For **clause** see GRAMMAR, p. 24, and the GLOSSARY.)
> (Non-S but common informally: There's no question but he'll be back by two.)
> At least with a dog there can be no question of disloyalty.
> In the mind of a ten-year-old there can be no question that two and two make four.

quite The standard formal meaning is *completely*, *positively*. **Quite** is commonly used informally to mean *fairly*, *rather*, but this should be avoided in formal written contexts.
> The guard suddenly realized that the last cell was now quite empty.
> Informal: The car engine was quite powerful, but the hill was evidently too steep for it.

quorum The standard plural is **quorums**.

quote in standard English is a verb only; the noun is **quotation**. **Quote** as a noun is part of the specialist vocabulary of commerce and printing.

> He read a short introductory quotation, then quoted the rest by heart.

R

raise, raze have opposed meanings, though they sound identical. The first means *elevate*, the second means *demolish, level to the ground*. The expression "raze to the ground" is therefore a tautology.

> He plans to raze the barn and raise a hostelry in its stead.

rapt, wrapped sound the same but have two quite different meanings. The first means *deeply involved* (the related noun is **rapture**), the second *enveloped*.

> She spoke not a word, apparently being rapt in thought.
>
> The snowshoes were wrapped in caribou hide.

reaction, response The first has connotations of spontaneity and rapidity which the second does not. The expression "immediate reaction" is tautologous.

> There was little reaction from the crowd when they heard the news.
>
> I wonder if we'll get any response before next year.
>
> (Non-S: I wonder if we'll get any reaction before next year.)

reason why is used with **that**, not **because**.

> The reason why he couldn't come was that he had flu.
>
> Better: The reason he couldn't come was that he had flu.
>
> (Non-S: The reason why he couldn't come was because he had flu.)

Tell me the reason why.

Better: Tell me the reason. Tell me why.

rebut, refute, repudiate The first refers to putting down an opponent's arguments or claims by countering with ones of your own. The second refers to showing an argument or claim to be invalid or wrong. The third means simply *deny*. They are commonly confused and misused: note that none is an exact synonym for any other.

Billy should rebut for our side in the debate.

I used my ticket stub to refute their allegations that I had been travelling under an assumed name.

The girl lost no time in roundly repudiating the merchant's claim to be an honest trader.

recoup, recover, recuperate The first may be either transitive, meaning *recompense for*, or intransitive, meaning *recover from a financial loss*. The second and third are roughly synonymous, meaning *get better*, though **recover** is often used figuratively, especially in reference to a financial loss.

I insist on recouping you for some of the expenses of our trip.

Hoping to recoup, he put all his money into heavy metals.

We threw an extra matinee in an attempt to recover some of our losses.

He is still recovering [or recuperating] from a bout of hepatitis.

recourse, resource, resort may be roughly synonymous but each has a different connotation. **Recourse** is used in reference to a possible source of help for a specific problem; **resort** is similar, but it also has connotations of being an extreme action. **Resource** is the most general of the three, referring to something or someone one can turn to when necessary.

You may have to have recourse to our files for further information.

As a last resort I decided to write a letter demanding action.

recumbent

    The resources of the local library have been enough for my work.

recumbent See **prone**.

redolent of means either *smelling of* or *suggestive of*.

    Badger's kitchen was redolent of freshly-baked bread.

    To me the black briefcase was redolent of boardrooms and high finance.

reduce See **deplete**.

redundancy usually refers to unnecessary words, though it may also be used in other contexts. See **pleonasm**.

refer See **allude**.

referendum The standard plural is **referendums**.

refute means *conclusively prove to be false*. See **rebut**.

regard as as a verb meaning *judge* is informally often followed by **being** or another similar participle. This is unnecessary in standard English.

    I regard her as the leading pianist of our time.

    (Non-S but common informally: I regard her as being the leading pianist of our time.)

(as) regards, in regard to, with regard to are standard. The phrase "in regards to" is not.

    As regards that last request, I think we'd better overlook it.

    We should write a letter in (or with) regard to the proposed land development.

(in the) region of An overworked cliché. Use **about** or **around** instead.

regretfully, regrettably The first means *with feelings of regret*. The second (which, unlike the first, is spelled with two *t*s) means *unfortunately*.

> He told me regretfully that he would soon be leaving Middleton.
>
> Regrettably, the most incriminating evidence was lost.

relate is a transitive verb meaning *tell* or *put in a relationship*. The intransitive **relate to** meaning *agree with*, *get on with* is commonly heard and seems to be becoming standard.

> He related what had happened to him in the village.
>
> Can you relate his figures to your results? Are they related?
>
> (Common except formally: I relate well with her. I can relate to that.)

relatively Do not use with words such as **percentage** or **proportion**, which themselves already include the concept of a part relative to a whole. Use **relatively** only if the notion of a whole is present. See also **comparatively**.

> It seemed a large amount, but I suppose it represented a relatively small part of his personal fortune.
>
> (Non-S: It was a relatively small proportion of the money.)

relevant means *pertinent*. It is used in a relative way: A is relevant to B. Nothing can be relevant in isolation.

> The matter of mousetraps is irrelevant to our discussion of leisure activities.

renege means *go back on an agreement*. It is intransitive, and should not be followed by **on** or any object.

> They decided to renege without consulting us first.
>
> (Non-S: They reneged on their agreement.)

repel, repulse, repulsive The first two mean *drive back opposing force* with the secondary meaning of *cause disgust in*. The third tends only to have the second meaning.

> Her cooking was so repulsive it repelled even the dog.

repudiate

By noon we had successfully repulsed the surprise attack.

repudiate Means *deny*. See **refute**.

repulse See **repel**.

resource, resort See **recourse**.

respectively Used to connect individual items in two lists at once. Avoid if at all possible: may easily confuse a reader.
John and Susan received a book and a ball respectively.
Clearer: John received a book and Susan a ball.

respite means *temporary relief*. The expression "temporary respite" is a tautology.

responsible for may mean *liable to be asked to account for*, *obliged to take care of*, or *being the cause of*. Be sure that your reader understands which of the three is intended.
He is responsible for seeing that the knives are kept sharpened.
She now felt responsible for feeding the local waifs and strays.
He admitted he was responsible for the noise we heard last night.

restaurateur Note spelling. Not "restauranteur"—there's a "rat" in the correct version.

restful, restive have quite opposite meanings. The first means *providing rest*, *peaceful*; the second, *unmanageable* or *fidgety*, *restless*.
I spent a restful weekend in the country.
This year's students have become increasingly restive.
The delay made the crowd restive and impatient.

revenge for, revenge on The first is passive, meaning *be given* *satisfaction or repayment for a wrong*; the second is active, meaning *repay a wrong in kind*. The noun is **revenge**. See also **avenge**.

I was revenged for the wrong he had done me.

The day when she could revenge herself on him was not long coming.

reverend, reverent The first means *worthy of reverence*, the second *showing piety or reverence*. See page 131 for abbreviation of the honorary title **Reverend**, used of certain members of the clergy. See also **venerate**, **worship**.

I would not presume to criticize such a reverend master.

The three women then crossed themselves reverently.

Here comes the Reverend Mr Stirling. (Informal only: Here comes Reverend Stirling.)

reversal, reversion The first means **turnabout**, the second **going back**. The corresponding verbs are **reverse** and **revert**.

The battle proved a reversal of his previous good fortune.

The reversion to Standard Time comes in autumn.

reverse See **contrary**.

reversion See **reversal**.

revert means *turn back*. The expression "revert back" is a tautology.

rostrum See **dais**.

S

sacrilege, sacrilegious have to do with the violation of something sacred. Note that these words do *not* include the word **religious**; in fact, they reverse the order of the latter's first two vowels.

sanction The verb means *approve or authorize* something, but the noun (often used with the verb **impose**) refers to coercive action on the part of one or more nations to change the political, commercial, or religious policies of another.

> I may be easygoing, but I can't possibly sanction such immorality.

> The sanctions imposed against the island nation included a ban on shipping.

sarcasm refers to a manner of saying one thing but clearly implying the opposite. It has bad overtones. See also **irony**.

scarcely X when Y Be sure that X and Y are grammatically equivalent. See also **hardly X when Y**.

> She had scarcely sat down when the pot began to boil over.

scenario may refer to the narrative development of a drama, a film script, or an imagined series of events.

> He staggered into the agent's office with an armload of scenarios.

> Their doomsday scenario also includes an outbreak of bubonic plague.

Scottish, Scotch, Scots The first is the standard general adjective for anything to do with Scotland or its people. The second is used only of particular items, such as Scotch broth or Scotch whisky. The third is used to describe its dialects of English, e.g. **Highland Scots**, as well as the identity of its people, e.g. Scotsman, Scotswoman. The Celtic language spoken in parts of Scotland and Nova Scotia is Scots Gaelic.

scrutiny means *close and careful examination*, so should not be preceded by redundant adjectives such as **close**, **careful** or **intense**.

seasonable, seasonal The first means *expectable, in keeping with the season*. The second means *happening at a particular season*.

On a seasonable summer's day we set off for the beach.

The seasonal migration of waterfowl reaches its peak in November.

second, secondly as adverbs mean *in second place*. The first is standard, unless you have already started your list with **firstly** (which itself has faintly pretentious overtones).

Second, we must be prepared to bear any burden to secure and maintain peace.

second [adjective]**est** Be sure you mean what you say.

Canada is the world's second largest country. Canada is the largest country in the world after the USSR.

(Wrong: Canada is the second largest country in the world after the USSR [implies that the USSR is second and Canada third].)

self-confessed is a tautology. The adjective **confessed** is enough.

He is a confessed gambling addict.

sensible, sensibility The usual meaning of the first is *showing common sense*, but it may also mean *sensitive, aware*. Context should make the intended meaning clear. The second word means *sensitivity, awareness*.

Her agent complimented her on having made a sensible decision.

He seemed hardly sensible of the words she spoke.

His paintings offended the sensibilities of some of the local worthies.

sensual, sensuous The first means *sexually arousing* and is frequently used in a negative sense. The second means *arousing response from any or all of the senses*.

Her costume had obviously been designed for maximum sensual impact.

His first visit to the pleasure palace was nothing like the sensuous experience he had dreamed of.

separate Note spelling—there's "a rat" in it.

serve, service The first as a verb means *wait on, carry out the wishes of*. The second means *maintain*.

> A computer network will serve the world university community.
>
> They taught themselves how to service the farm machinery.

several, various The first may be either a pronoun (followed by **of**) or an adjective meaning *more than two but not many*. The second is an adjective meaning *several or many*.

> The priest wrote several [adj.] pleading letters to several [pron.] of his parishioners.
>
> The priest wrote pleading letters to various parishioners.
>
> (Non-S: The priest wrote pleading letters to various of his parishioners.)

shall/will Standard English future tense is **shall** with **I** and **we**, and **will** with all other personal pronouns. The reverse occurs when these words are used to express determination, not futurity. The conditional forms of **shall** and **will** are **should** and **would**, though in American **would** is commonly used throughout. Dialect use of **shall** and **will** varies the world over. In informal written English the contraction -**'ll** may be used in place of either **shall** or **will**.

> I shall be taking the car into town tomorrow. We shall meet him there.
>
> Will you be coming with us? Marty will but Emma won't. They'll be at school.
>
> "I will be heard!" someone cried from the back of the courtroom.
>
> "You shall sit down and be quiet at once," ordered the judge sternly.
>
> I'm sure I should [Amer. would] have seen him if he had been there. He would have been easy to spot.

shameless, shameful In spite of their opposite looks, these two words are near-synonyms. The first means *having no personal shame*, and is applied to persons. The second means *causing shame*, and is usually applied to acts or objects.

Gertrude was known to be a shameless gossip.

Even more shameful was Mary's treatment of her parents.

should/would See **shall/will** above.

sic is Latin for *thus*. It is placed in brackets after a quoted word or words which appear wrong or defective to show that the quotation is accurate.

The composer wrote that his "pianny" [sic] needed a tune.

sick See **ill, sick**.

since [specified time] means *from [specified time] and still continuing*. A present-tense auxiliary (e.g. "has") + past participle is needed.

He has been our accountant since 1982.

(Non-S: He was our accountant since 1982.)

situation means *location* or *combination of circumstances*. Avoid preceding it with words such as **crisis**, **job** or **work** which in themselves already imply some kind of situation.

The bank manager quizzed Mildred about the financial situation at work.

sleight, slight The first, a noun, means *skill*, and is usually only found in reference to sleight of hand (conjuring). The second is an adjective meaning *insignificant, thin*.

so meaning *therefore* and used to join two shorter sentences may or may not be preceded by **and**. Use a comma.

He asked me to come, so I did.

They had already gone to bed, and so he bedded down in the hayloft.

so-called

so-called is almost always used ironically. Be certain your reader understands if this is not intended.

> "My so-called husband hasn't been seen for six days," she retorted caustically.

> (Ambiguous: In 1982 a so-called University for Peace was built in Costa Rica.)

solecism Non-standard grammar or usage. See more under **pleonasm**.

sometime, some time The first is an adverb. The second is an adjective + noun combination.

> Why not plan to visit us sometime this summer?

> He said he would need some time in which to prepare a statement.

sort of See **kind of**.

spate means *flood (of river)*. It is sometimes mistakenly thought to mean *flurry of activity*.

> The river was in full spate when I reached the dock.

> (Non-S: Spring usually brings a spate of engagement parties.)

speciality, specialty The first is British, the second American.

spoonfuls is standard, not "spoonsful" or "spoons full" (unless the spoons themselves are to be included). (Compare with hyphenated personal constructions such as passer-by and sister-in-law, whose plural forms are passers-by and sisters-in-law.)

> He then added two spoonfuls of chopped herbs to the marinade.

stanch, staunch The first is a verb meaning *stop the flow from*. The second is an adjective meaning *firm, loyal*.

They tried to stanch severely bleeding wounds with torn-up
    sheets.

He is a staunch friend.

standard English See **dialect, jargon, lingua franca**.

starving means *dying from lack of food*, though it is commonly
used in a jocular sense to mean *extremely hungry*. The expression "starving to death" is, strictly speaking, tautological.

state as a verb means *declare or explain fully*. It is not merely a
synonym for **say** or **remark**.

The judge asked him to state his name and occupation.
(Non-S: "You took a long time," the old man stated.)

stationary, stationery The first is an adjective meaning *unmov-
ing*. The second is a collective noun referring to writing or
office requisites such as paper, envelopes, ledger books, ink,
and paper clips.

straight, strait The first is an adjective or adverb meaning *not
bent or curved* or *directly*. The second is an adjective (which is
also commonly used as a noun) meaning *tight* or *narrow*.

He won the prize for painting the straightest line.
I want you to come straight home.
Are strait-jackets still used in hospitals nowadays?
His cottage overlooked the Northumberland Strait.

strata is plural and means *levels*. The singular is **stratum**.

student body has pretentious overtones. Use **students** instead.

style may be combined, using a hyphen, with an adjective.
The resultant word is itself an adjective. This usage is mainly
informal.

The local police were trained in the basics of CIA-style
    coups.

suasion See **persuasion**.

substitute X for Y means *put X in place of Y*. Notice that it means the opposite of **replace X with Y**.

>   You could substitute the oil you have for the butter you lack.
>   (Non-S: She had substituted her usual dress for a business suit.)

such as See **like**.

supersede does *not* contain "cede" even though it sounds as though it should. The word is related to the Latin *sedere*, meaning *sit*, and literally means *sit above (something else)*.

>   The mechanical slide rule was largely superseded by the electronic calculator.

supine refers to lying on your spine. See **prone**.

surrounded means *completely encircled*, so it is non-standard to speak of something as being partly surrounded. The expression "completely surrounded" is a tautology.

T

take place See **occur**.

tautology is an expression that contains unnecessary words, such as "He is an unmarried bachelor." See **pleonasm**.

terms of See **in terms of**.

than When used to link two items that are being compared, be sure that they are grammatically equivalent. If in doubt, expand to repeat all words in the second item.

>   I live nearer town than my brother does.
>   I live nearer to the town than to my brother.

Ambiguous: I live nearer town than my brother.
You like reading more than (you like) me.
You like reading more than I (like reading).

that, what, which, who The first is the restrictive relative pronoun, used of both personal and impersonal objects. **Which** and **who** are the non-restrictive impersonal and personal forms. **What** is the interrogative impersonal form; **who** is its personal equivalent. (See GRAMMAR, p. 22.)

The book that I borrowed yesterday is missing. The man that I saw in my office later may have taken it.
Alice in Wonderland, which I borrowed yesterday, is missing. John Snodgrass, who was in my office later, may have taken it.
He asked me what I had done. "What have you done?" he asked.
He asked me who was at the door. "Who is at the door?" he asked.

their, there, they're sound the same, so are often confused, even, at times, by experienced writers. **Their** is the possessive adjective, **there** is an adverb, and **they're** is the abbreviation for **they are**.

They're supposed to put their books there.

then is usually an adverb meaning *at that time*. It may also function as an adjective, being placed before the relevant noun.

He was then [adverb] the Prime Minister.
They asked the then [adjective] Prime Minister.

think to oneself A tautological expression. Omit the last two words.

"Something must be done," she thought.
(Non-S: "Something must be done," she thought to herself.)

this when used as a pronoun may be ambiguous. Guard

against this, repeating the reference if necessary to avoid confusion.

> Ambiguous: The student nonchalantly left half the test-tubes unwashed and did not turn off the exhaust fan; this especially infuriated Carruthers. (Was it the nonchalance, not washing the test-tubes, leaving the fan on, or all three that especially infuriated him?)

though See **although**.

through used in the sense of *up to and including* is American only. **From . . . to** is the acceptable equivalent, even in the USA.

> Most adults work from Monday to Friday.
> American: Most adults work Monday through Friday.

till, until are interchangeable in standard English. The spellings "'till" and "'til" are non-standard.

time is not needed after nouns which themselves are units of time.

> I expect to see him in two weeks.
> (Non-S: I expect to see him in two weeks' time.)

tirade See **harangue**.

together with See **along with**.

ton, tonne There are two kinds of ton, a long ton weighing 2,240 pounds, and a short ton weighing 2,000 pounds. A metric tonne weighs 1,000 kilograms (which, as it happens, is just 36 pounds short of being a long ton).

tortuous, torturous The first means *twisting* or *devious*. The second means *involving torture*.

> I could not follow the tortuous plot of her last novel.

The president's torturous methods finally provoked a public
outcry.

total of The expression "the total of [number]" takes a singular
verb; "a total of [number]" is followed by a plural verb. See
also **number of**.
The total of 186 deaths is [singular] regarded as excessive.
A total of 3500 ducats were [plural] paid to the duke's
daughter.

toward, towards The first is preferred in American usage, the
second in British. Either is acceptable in standard English.

trans[geographical name] No hyphen or capital is needed
when the second element is the name of a physical entity, such
as the Alps or the Atlantic: the correct forms are transalpine
and transatlantic. A hyphen and a capital are both used when
trans- is linked to a political entity such as Canada: trans-Can-
adian.

transpire strictly means *become known, leak out*. Informally
it is often used as a synonym for *happen*, but this should be
avoided in formal usage.
It transpired that the decision had been made three weeks
earlier.
(Non-S but common informally: I wonder what transpired
when he found his precious cup gone.)

treble, triple Apart from the specialized musical term "treble
clef" both have to do with the number three. The first as a
general adjective is preferable for amount; the second for
kinds. **Treble** is the standard verb, though **triple** is commonly
heard.
He had no idea of how he was to bear the treble burden
[three times as heavy] of the new family.
This is really a kind of triple problem [having three parts].

triumphal, triumphant

> The board has already decided to treble the manager's salary.

triumphal, triumphant The first means *pertaining to a victory or other triumph*; the second, *exultant*.

> At the main square the citizens had constructed a triumphal arch.
> He returned to the kitchen with a triumphant smile on his face.

trivia is plural. The singular is **triviality**.

> How can you possibly remember all these trivia?
> It's a triviality.

true facts is either a tautology or incorrect. Omit the first word.

try to meaning *attempt* is standard. "Try and" is informal only.

> Try to get some sleep.
> (Non-S but common informally: Try and get some sleep.)

turbid, turgid The first means *muddy, mixed-up*, the second *swollen, inflated*.

> The evidence was soon swept away by the turbid river.
> His turgid speech brought pained expressions to many faces.

U

undoubtedly See **doubtless**.

unequivocal means *clear, unmistakable*. The adverb is **unequivocally**. (The forms "unequivocable" and "unequivocably" are sometimes heard, but they are non-standard.)

> It seemed to me that his answer was quite unequivocal.

unexceptionable, unexceptional The first means *acceptable*; the second, *commonplace*. See **exceptionable**.

It seems he viewed his son's shameful conduct as unexceptionable.

Much of Wordsworth's poetry is unexceptional.

unique means *one of a kind*. Something is either unique or it is not. The expressions "more unique" and "very unique" are literal nonsense.

unlike is similar to **like** in that it must refer to a noun or pronoun. It may not refer to a clause. Be sure that the two entities being compared are grammatically and idiomatically equivalent. See **like**.

He insisted on paying in advance, unlike his father.

(Non-S: He paid in advance, unlike his father had ever done [clause].)

(Non-S: He paid in advance, unlike the times when his father had been in charge [second subject not equivalent to first].)

unpractical See **impractical**.

until and **till** (not "'til" or "'till") are both standard. See **till**.

up is redundant in such colloquial expressions as

tighten up	eat up	drink up	lift up
buoy up	loosen up	phone up	ring up
climb up	mix up	gather up	freeze up.

upon and **on** are often equivalent. See **on**.

usage, use Both mean *habit, custom*, though **use** has many more meanings. **Usage** is generally limited to discussions of grammar or church ritual.

use, utilize are roughly synonymous verbs. It might be as well to reserve the second for situations involving some kind of ingenuity.

Will you be using the hacksaw this afternoon?

Somehow she had managed to utilize every square inch of the walls of the small cabin.

V

various meaning *several or many different* is an adjective, and should therefore not be followed by **of**. The expression "various different [plural noun]" is a tautology. See **several**.

venal, venial The first means *bribable, corruptible*; the second, *pardonable*.

The mayor was known to be the town's most venal official.

Should the sin of gluttony be accepted as venial, as long as children starve in this world?

venerate, worship The first means *regard with respect and reverence*; the second, *revere as a supernatural being or power*. Gurus and saints are venerated; gods are worshipped. See also **reverend, reverent**.

vengeance See **avenge**.

venial See **venal**.

verbal refers to something concerned with words in general (or verbs in particular). It is often used as an informal synonym for **oral** in expressions like "verbal communication" or "verbal contract" but this usage is strictly non-standard. See **oral**.

verge on, verge to The first means *border on*, the second *approach, incline towards*.

For three weeks his finances verged on bankruptcy.

They seem to be verging to a declaration of war.

very Avoid over-using this word to intensify a worn-out adjective. Find a stronger adjective.

via means *by way of [a particular place]*. It is often used informally to mean *by means of [a particular person or thing]*, but this is regarded as non-standard.

> We drove from Chicago to Montreal via Detroit and Toronto.
>
> (Non-S: I'll send it to you via my son. The message was delivered via telegraph.)

viable means *capable of life, able to exist independently*. It is frequently used as a loose synonym for **workable**, but this usage is not standard.

> In less than a year they established a viable farming community.
>
> (Non-S: It didn't seem like a very viable way to rob a bank.)

virtually means *almost*. See also **practically**.

vivid means *bright, striking*. See also **livid, lurid**.

vortex Both **vortexes** and **vortices** are standard plurals.

W

want See **need**.

was, were are past tense forms of the irregular verb **be**. The usual first and third person singular form is (I, he, she, it) **was**, but this changes to **were** if it occurs in an imaginary or hypothetical context. This changed form of the verb is known as the **subjunctive mood**, and it is an important aspect of many other European languages. Use of the subjunctive in English appears to be generally fading, however, though usage varies throughout the world. Today, an American is probably more likely than a British English-speaker to use the subjunctive in a conditional context such as "I would do it if I were manager (but I'm not)," or "I wish that he were here (but he's not)." The best one can do is be guided by local educated usage. Here are some further idiomatic usages showing the distinction in effect between subjunctive and ordinary (indicative) forms:

I didn't even notice if he was [definitely, and at a specific time in the past] asleep.

If he were to sleep there, he would be warm enough [hypothetical condition dependent on a still unrealized suggestion].

If I were you, I'd keep out of it [hypothetical condition; as I'm not you].

If I was [at a specific time in the past] an idiot to run, you were a fool to stay.

well is the adverbial form of **good**. Its antonym is **badly**. See **good, goodly**.

She played well, but I fared badly.

well- A hyphen is used to join **well** to an adjective when they precede a noun. There is no hyphen when **well** + adjective follows the noun.

It was a well-rehearsed act. The act had been well rehearsed.

Welsh is the word applied to the Celtic language spoken in parts of Wales. It is related to Irish and Scots Gaelic, Breton (the language of Brittany), and the ancient tongues of Cornish (Cornwall) and Manx (Isle of Man).

what is an impersonal interrogative pronoun. See **that, what, which, who,** also GRAMMAR (p. 22).

whence means *from where*. Do not precede with *from*.

whether or not. The last two words are not needed if all you mean is *if*. They are needed, however, if there is a clear choice of alternatives.

I doubt whether he can get there in time.

I need to know whether you intend to help us or not.

which is the non-restrictive impersonal relative pronoun. See **that, what, which, who,** also GRAMMAR (p. 22).

My rheumatism, which had been quiescent for some months, suddenly flared up.

while literally means *during the time that*, but it may also be used figuratively to mean *although*, as long as no ambiguity results. It is not a general synonym for **and** or **but.** See also **awhile**.

While I admire his principles, I cannot approve of his methods.

(Non-S: The days are warm, while the nights are cool.)

(Non-S: He asked me to go, while I had something else to do.)

who is the non-restrictive personal relative pronoun, as well as the personal interrogative pronoun. See **that, what, which, who**; also GRAMMAR (p. 22).

Old Robie Long, who lives down on the corner, came to call this afternoon.

who, whom Usage experts are divided on what constitutes standard procedure in the use of these words. The standard approach is to use **whom** as the object of a preposition or a verb, and **who** everywhere else. A test: substitute **he** for **who** and **him** for **whom.** Which sounds right? See also **whoever**.

To whom shall I send the invitation [object of preposition]?

Whom shall I call first [object of verb]?

whoever

Did Billy, who they thought was dead, eventually escape [subject of verb "was"]?

whoever serves as both subjective and objective case. [The old objective form "whomever" is not now generally used.]

Whoever [subject] speaks first may have it.

Give it to whoever [object] speaks first.

whose may refer to either persons or things. If it begins a parenthetical clause, then parenthetical commas (see TYPOGRAPHY, pp. 136–7) must be included; if not, not. See also **that, what, which, who**.

The oldest elm, whose leaves had already begun to fall [parenthetical], was attacked by grubs.

Students whose assignments have already been handed in [non-parenthetical] may now leave.

will, would When used in future constructions, the first implies certainty, the second possibility. Maintain one or the other at least to the end of a paragraph before switching.

A shuttle service to the city will run every hour [certainty].

A shuttle service to the city would run every hour [if conditions were to make this possible].

-wise This suffix, meaning *in the manner of*, occurs in combination with a few long-established English nouns, and has the effect of transforming them into adverbs. Informally, **-wise** may also be used as though it added *concerning* or *about* to the noun which it follows. This is non-standard, however.

Turn the screw clockwise.

(Non-S: I have to get down to work, studywise.)

womankind is the feminine equivalent of **mankind**. "Womenkind" is not a standard English form.

worship See **venerate**.

worthwhile, worth while Use the first form when it precedes a noun and is used as an adjective. Use the second form when it follows a noun + predicate. (Best of all is to use a stronger word.)

I'm sure you'll all agree that this is a worthwhile cause.

You'll all agree that this cause is worth while.

would See **will**.

wrapped See **rapt**.

write Standard English places **to** after this verb when it means *write a letter*, though informally the **to** tends to be omitted.

Be sure you write to your mother.

(Non-S: Be sure you write your mother.)

Y

yes Treat either as a direct quotation (with opening capital) or as a non-capitalized word which is not a direct quotation. See also **no**.

His answer was, "Yes, I will." His answer was yes, he would.

Yiddish is a European Jewish language, based on medieval German but conventionally written in the Hebrew alphabet. **Hebrew**, the Semitic language of the Old Testament, is related to Arabic. It was revived earlier this century to become the official language of Israel.

Z

zenith means *highest point*. The **nadir** is the lowest point.

zoom means *climb steeply*. It is often used informally to mean *move horizontally rapidly*. It should not be used as a synonym for words such as **plunge** or **swoop** which denote downward motion.

Typography

There is little difference between American and British terminology and usage when it comes to the non-verbal conventions of printed and written English. The most notable difference is that in American terminology the dot at the end of a sentence is called a *period*, while in British the dot is a *full stop*. To avoid possible confusion, I'm going to use another long-established term, **point**, for both. (See more below, under **point**.) The only significant difference between American and British convention is in the use of quotation marks, and this is explained under **quotation marks**.

Other conventions, such as those of abbreviations, capital letters, hyphens, italics and numerals, are also non-verbal. All are included in this chapter. The whole thing is arranged alphabetically by subject or term.

abbreviations
1. Many abbreviations end with a point, but this is not necessary if the last letter of the word is included in the abbreviation. Americans usually include the point, however. For further guidance see the Index.

B.A.   T. S. Eliot   Dec.   Wed.   p. (page)   pp. (pages)
mi. (mile)   in. (inch)   lb. (pound)
Amer.: Dr.   Mr.   Mrs.   St. (street or saint)   Ave.   Rev.
Brit.: Dr   Mr   Mrs   St (street or saint)   Ave   Revd

Points are not needed after metric abbreviations such as

g (gram)   mg (milligram)   kg (kilogram)
cm (centimeter, -re*)   l (liter, -re)   km (kilometer, -re)

* The first spelling is American; the second, British.

2. Points are not normally needed in sequences of capitals, or in numerical abbreviations.

UN BBC BC AD UNESCO PLO USA USSR UK
C (Celsius)   F (Fahrenheit)   1st   2nd   3rd

3. No point is needed if the abbreviation itself is used colloquially.

demo(nstration)   trig(onometry)   vac(ation)
co-op(erative)

See your dictionary for further information.

ampersand A typographical sign meaning *and*. (The term is supposed to come from "and *per se* and"—literally "and in itself and".) The ampersand is rarely used in formal writing other than where it already appears in names of business firms. In poetry and in informally rendered speech, it may be used to show use of the spoken contraction "'n" commonly used to link a pair of words:

Boosey & Hawkes
ham & eggs (informal)

The ampersand is also used in one of the two abbreviations for *et cetera*: &c. (The more usual abbreviation is etc.)

apostrophe
1. An apostrophe may be used after a noun, usually with the letter *s*, to indicate possession:

Anitra's dance   James's ladder   a tree's leaves

The same form is used with indefinite pronouns:

somebody's handbag   someone else's worry   other people's views

If the noun is a plural already ending in *s*, the apostrophe follows the end of the word:

   a Scouts' Jamboree   the lions' den   the ladies' hats

Plural nouns which do not end in *s* are treated as though singular:

   a children's playground   the men's room

As a rule, this form is used only with living things. We do not normally speak of *a house's floor* or *the book's cover*, but *the floor of a house* or *the cover of the book*. Also note that in titles such as Girls School, Teamsters Union, and Womens Institute, the first word is descriptive rather than possessive, and no apostrophe is needed.

(In spoken English a plural form, such as *the lions' den*, may sound exactly like the singular: *the lion's den*. Unless it is already clear that you mean more than one lion, it is better to rephrase to avoid any ambiguity: *the den of the lions*.)

If a group together possesses something in common, the apostrophe comes at the end of the group:

   John and Mary's mother
   the Hatfields and McCoys' feud

Possessive pronouns such as *his*, *hers*, *its*, *yours* and *theirs* have no apostrophe:

   The orange hat is hers.   The horse had lost its bridle.
   Is that car yours or theirs? No, it's his.

2. An apostrophe may indicate that letters have been omitted from a word (usually an auxiliary verb, a pronoun, or *not*). Some examples:

   it's=it is   there's=there is   who's=who is/has
   won't=will not   mustn't=must not
   shouldn't=should not   you're=you are
   let's=let us   'twas=it was   I've=I have
   he's=he is/has   she'd=she had

brackets (square brackets)

These forms, called **contractions**, are perfectly acceptable in informal written and spoken English, but are usually best avoided in formal writing. *Beware of the following often confused distinctions!*

1. *its* (no apostrophe)=*belonging to it*, e.g. *its bridle, its food*. *it's* (contraction with apostrophe)=*it is*. *It's time to go*.
The same rule applies to *theirs* and *there's*, and *whose* and *who's*.

2. Use singular and plural apostrophes correctly in expressions such as

a hard day's work   seven months' hard work
the year's events   two weeks' holiday.

3. No apostrophe is needed in plural forms such as

the Smiths   the Joneses   the 1920s   cross your *t*s

unless the plural is itself possessive:

the Smiths' house
the Joneses' car (as opposed to Miss Jones's car).

brackets (square brackets) These show when material has been added to an original text by someone else, such as an editor.

"Five years later [actually, it was in 1797, which was six years later] our first son was born."
"[The landowners] have finally banded together." (The original text might have had "they" or something rude.)

capital letters

1. A capital letter begins every sentence, including uncompleted sentences and sentences that are quoted.

When will he come? In half an hour, I think.
"When will he come?" my father asked.
I answered, "In half an hour, I think."

2. Capitalize all proper nouns (or their abbreviations), and usually all adjectives derived from proper nouns.

Gerard Manley Hopkins   New England   Asian.

3. Capitalize a title if it is used as part of someone's name.

Doctor Doolittle   Aunt Rhoda   Mother
Miss Julia   Professor Simms
Sir Christopher Downes
Uncle Bert   Grandfather   Archbishop Laval

4. Capitalize common nouns such as *building*, *company*, *lake*, *street*, or *university* when they are part of a title.

Chrysler Building   Associated Book Company
Crystal Lake   Oxford Street
Fleetmore University

5. Capitalize the first word and all other lexical words in the titles of books, plays, poems, magazines, newspapers, stories, reports and other articles. Note: the title of a whole volume (book, magazine or newspaper) should be in italics (or underlined), while titles of individual articles, stories, or poems should be in quotation marks. See also **italics** and **quotation marks**.

Poe's "The Raven" Stockton's "The Lady or the Tiger?"
Hemingway's *A Farewell to Arms*   *The Economist*

(Note: If the word "the" is part of the title of a periodical, do not capitalize or italicize it when it occurs as part of a sentence: Have you read the *Economist* this week? What does the *New York Times* have to say about the strike?)

6. Always capitalize *I* and *O*. (see VOCABULARY, under **O, oh**.)

7. Capitalize abstract nouns when they are personified (addressed as persons) or particularized.

Why, O Love, are you absent from my life?
Through the valleys Spring came singing joyfully.

colon

> The Queen will address the Senate later this week [a
> particular monarch and political body are
> understood].

colon

1. A colon may join two clauses into a sentence that conveys
the idea of some kind of logical relationship, e.g. cause and
effect. It is commonly found in proverbial expressions.

> Marry in haste: repent at leisure.
> To err is human: to forgive, divine.

2. It may show that some kind of list or series is about to
begin.

> Australia has one island state: Tasmania.
> Most children have heard of them: Wynkyn, Blynkyn,
> and Nod.

The part of the sentence before the colon should be grammatically complete in itself. So it is incorrect to write

> Most children have heard of: Wynkyn, Blynkyn, and
> Nod.

comma

1. Commas separate non-essential, or parenthetical,
material from the rest of a sentence.

> My father, who had been in bed for weeks, suddenly
> announced that he could eat a horse.
> The old oak, which had been slowly dying for years,
> blew over in the storm.
> His wife, Gertrude, rarely washes her greasy hair.

Notice that two commas are necessary, one to mark the
beginning of the non-essential material, the other to mark the
end of it. A frequent mistake is to omit one of the two commas.
The test is that the sentence should still make complete sense
with the material between the commas left out.

Here are some examples of sentences where all the information is essential and where commas must therefore not be used.

Dogs that have been properly trained will sit on
command.
The man that attacked her was almost certainly a
stranger.
She will produce Genet's play *The Balcony* later this
month.

Whereas non-essential clauses are introduced with **who** (persons) or **which** (everything else), essential clauses may always be introduced with **that**.

2. Commas are used to separate items in a list of three or more.

He is studying chemistry, physics, and biology this year.
(The final comma of a list is often omitted, but it is possible for such an omission to be the cause of ambiguity or misunderstanding. It's safer and easier always to include it.)

3. A comma may precede *and* when short independent clauses are combined into one sentence.

The cats were screaming to be fed, and the dog had
run off after the schoolchildren.
John got up and left early, and I stayed in bed.

A comma is not needed if the subject or predicate in the shorter sentences is the same.

Mary combed her hair and then splashed cold water on
her face.
The cat fed six of her kittens and I fed the seventh.

Very short simple sentences may be combined without commas.

The sun rose and the birds began to sing.

4. Commas may be used to set off an aside.

Tell me, John, what made you come here?
I'm certain, however, that we have nothing to lose.
I want to have the kitchen painted, oh, let's say yellow.

5. A comma may be placed between two adjectives when each of them qualifies a noun in the same way.

He was a caring, loving (=caring and loving) father.

However, a comma is not used between two adjectives which qualify the noun in different ways, or when the first adjective affects the second rather than the noun.

Sands was a daring foreign correspondent (does not mean "daring and foreign").
We live in a dark blue bungalow (does not mean "dark and blue").

6. Use a comma to avoid possible ambiguity (or, better still, rewrite the sentence to get rid of the problem).

From the hills above, the town looked like a magic
kingdom.

7. A comma follows a participial or verbless clause.

Having waved goodbye, she turned to go inside.
His dinner over, John went to the piano.

8. A comma introduces direct speech (see **quotation marks**) and follows the salutation of a letter (see WRITING LETTERS AND OTHER PIECES, p. 160).

A sentence with too many commas should be rewritten.

dash

1. A long dash (the printer's term is an em rule) may mark a sudden break in the progression of a sentence. If the sentence is resumed, a second dash will show where this occurs. A common mistake is to use a comma instead of the second dash.

His mother always told me—oh, you've probably heard
the story anyway.

A workman—I can't remember his name—had
reported seeing someone.

(Non-S: A workman—I can't remember his name, had
reported seeing someone.)

2. In informal writing a dash may be used in place of a colon
to introduce a list.

There's nothing surer—the rich get rich and the poor
get poorer.

3. A short dash (technically called an en rule) is used to
join words where the words *to* or *against* are understood to be
missing, as well as to show joint authorship (as opposed to a
double-barrelled name):

the 1914–1918 war   the Portland–Newark flight
the Louis–Walcott match   the Smith–Jones theory

Typists: for a long dash type SPACE, HYPHEN, HYPHEN,
SPACE. For a short dash type SPACE, HYPHEN, SPACE.* See
also **hyphen** and **typing**.

dates In the USA (and sometimes in Canada), the month is
written first, then the day, then the year. Everywhere else in
the world (including non-English-speaking nations), the order
is day, month, year. This can cause untold confusion if you
are trying to decipher abbreviations such as 6.5.65 and are not
sure which of the two conventions has been used. To avoid
all possibility of misunderstanding, always use letters for the
month rather than a number. The standard forms are

American: December 6, 1979 *or* Dec. 6, 1979
Elsewhere: 6 December 1979 *or* 6 Dec. 1979

---

* A printer may not use spaces on either side of either an em or an en rule
(none are used in this book, for example), but typists need this means of
distinguishing between short dashes, which have spaces, and hyphens, which
do not.

ellipsis

ellipsis See **point**.

exclamation mark

1. An exclamation mark follows an exclamatory sentence, or an interjection.

> What a happy day it was!
> How happy I am!
> Who cares!   Ow!

2. It may also be used, in direct speech with imperative verbs, to show strong emotion or urgency.

> Sit down!
> Leave this house at once!

3. Editors sometimes use exclamation points inside brackets to show their disagreement or surprise with something quoted.

> The composer wrote his father that "a full four
> hundred [!] ladies of the night" had attended the
> dress rehearsal.

Exclamation points may often have been used in informal writing to give greater drama or immediacy to simple statements (this is especially true of comic-strip speech, advertising copy, and Queen Victoria's diaries), but this is non-standard.

full stop See **point**.

hyphen

1. Hyphens may be used to link separate words into something that functions as a single word:

> an empty-headed (adj.) dolt an open-air (adj.) concert
> a good-for-nothing (noun)   a Johnny-come-lately (noun)

Careful placing of hyphens may resolve possible ambiguities:

non-English speakers (speakers who do not orate in
English)
non-English-speakers (people who do not converse in
English)

There is no consistent rule about this; the wisest course is to
check your dictionary.

2. Hyphens are used to separate certain prefixes from the
nouns they modify (*ex-* is a common example), especially when
the prefix ends and the root-word begins with the same vowel.
They are also used to separate prefixes from nouns that begin
with a capital (see VOCABULARY, under **trans-**), or to distinguish the [prefix+root] form from a similarly spelled word
with a different meaning.

ex-president   co-operate   pro-Arab
re-creation (something created again)
recreation (leisure)

3. Hyphens may be used to show a common second element
in a list. The second element is given only at the end of the list.
(The technical term for this is **suspensive hyphen**.)

The room was full of three-, four-, and five-year-olds.

4. Hyphens are used to show that the word at the end of a
line is broken at the end of a syllable (usually for reasons of
space), and continues on the next line. British and American
conventions about breaking words differ. British hyphenation
is based on the etymology of the word, while American is conventionally based on typography.

Word-processing programs with automatic hyphenation
features are by no means infallible, and have even been known
to break up one-syllable words. Always be guided by your dictionary in deciding where to break a word.

italics In typing or writing, italics are indicated by underlining the words. They may denote:

1. titles of books, plays, journals, magazines

Great Expectations, Macbeth, London Review, Ebony.

2. foreign words which are not taken as part of standard English

It was one of those unsettling *déjà vu* experiences.

3. unusual speech stress (in informal writing)

I'm the one he should have seen (I and no one else).
I'm the one *he* should have seen (he should have seen
   me, not I him).

numbers Numbers may be represented either by words or figures. In general, we use words in formal or literary writing, figures in technical writing, and a mixture of the two in informal writing.

1. Figures are commonly used for
   a. any large or complicated number (2,719,734),
   b. statistics (an unemployment rate of 4 per cent),
   c. numbers grouped to suggest comparison (I spent 18 minutes eating dinner, David spent 14 minutes, and Michael only 12 minutes),
   d. decimals (3.1416),
   e. street addresses and postal codes (114 Minerva Drive),
   f. book references (Chapter 3, pp. 224–67),
   g. certain expressions of time (7:45 p.m.),
   h. dates (excluding the month) (June 2, 1982, or 2 June 1982), and
   i. large or complicated sums of money ($345.67, £891.05).

2. Words are commonly used for
   a. all expressions of number in formal letters (e.g. invitations) (Monday, the thirteenth of April, at seven o'clock p.m.),

b. numbers that begin a sentence (Seventy-seven guests were there),

c. sums that are less than a dollar or a pound (The light bulb cost thirty-eight pence, roughly equivalent to half a dollar),

d. any amount of money written in on a bank draft, money order, or other banking document (in addition to the representation in figures), and

e. any amount of money used as an adjective (a five-cent stamp, a tenpenny chocolate bar, a seven-dollar tie, a fifty-pound fine).

parentheses are always used in pairs.

1. They may show asides made by the writer.

Father Jones (who has just had his eightieth birthday) asked about you.

2. They may be used to insert extra information.

An interrogative sentence (question) then follows.
The last movement of the symphony is marked *Vivace* (lively).

3. They may surround reference numbers or letters:

(3a) Development of character.

period See **point**.

point (American **period**, British **full stop**)

1. A point closes all sentences, unless they are questions or exclamations. The next word normally begins with a capital letter.

2. A point closes abbreviations, unless their last letter is included in the abbreviation. (See **abbreviations**, above.) If such a point comes at the end of a sentence, it also marks the close of the sentence.

The room was full of furniture, clothes, dishes, etc.

3. For points at the end of quotations, see **quotation marks**.

4. Three points (. . .) indicate that material has been omitted. This is sometimes called an **ellipsis**. An ellipsis at the end of a sentence follows the point that marks the close of the sentence.

> His letter claims that "Many . . . are sick and tired of
> these games." [shows the original statement had some
> words which have been omitted]
> Perhaps if we were to try again. . . .

Typists: for an ellipsis, type space, point, point, point, space. The end of a sentence is always followed by *two* spaces, so a closing ellipsis is point, point, point, point, space, space. See **typing**.

question mark ends a direct query. Enclosed in parentheses, it shows doubt about a fact, number, or word.

> How?   What is it?   Tallis was born in 1505 (?).

quotation marks Two different conventions are at work here. They are sometimes called British and American, though in fact elements of both are in common use everywhere. For example, a majority of the world's English-language publishers, including many British publishers, use double quotation marks to enclose quotations. The conventions outlined here are familiar to English readers the world over.

1. Use double quotation marks to enclose words which are quoted directly from some other source. Anything quoted within that quotation should be in single quotation marks.

> "I don't think I 'should know better'," Jim remarked.

2. Punctuation which is logically part of the quoted material should remain within the quotation. Closing punctuation which is not part of the quoted material should go after the closing quotation marks. (Note: American convention is to put any final points or commas *before* the closing quotation marks, whether logically part of the quoted material or not.)

We all gathered in the barn for a typical "hoedown".
Amer.: We all gathered in the barn for a "hoedown."
"That", he said, "is an excellent idea."
Amer.: "That," he said, "is an excellent idea."

3. Generally, only one of the standard closing punctuation
marks (point, question mark, exclamation mark) may occur at
the end of a sentence (whether before or after a closing quotation mark). But note two exceptions: an embedded question
or exclamation requires its own punctuation; and titles of
books, plays, or films always retain their original punctuation.
If the sentence thereby looks unusual or ridiculous, rewrite it.

Children often ask, "Where do I come from?"
Can you think why she asked, "Where may I catch
the bus?"?
Who is the author of *Westward Ho!*?

4. A point at the end of a quotation is replaced by a comma
when the sentence continues beyond the quotation. Question
marks and exclamation marks are not affected in this way.

"I am tired of life," she said [comma replaces point].
"How delighted I am to see you!" she cried.
"Where may I catch the bus?" she asked.

5. Quotation marks surround the titles of articles, chapters
of books, short works not published separately (e.g. poems and
short stories), and songs. (See also **italics**, above.)

That was the year in which "Blue Moon" became
popular.
"Grandma's Legacy" is included in *A Family Zoo*.

It is clear that much could be done to standardize English
conventions of quotation. Meanwhile, the best procedure is to
choose a system and stick to it. Most readers can get used to
anything more easily than inconsistency, particularly in such
mechanical matters as punctuation.

semi-colon

1. joins clauses without any conjunction being needed.

He went up to bed; I, on the other hand, continued my
   reading.

2. precedes a conjunctive adverb (which is then followed by
a comma).

The place is a mess; moreover, I have nothing to eat.

3. functions as a strong comma.

The old man, who had been staring at me, finally
   began to advance; and it was just then the clock
   struck twelve, all the factory whistles of the town
   began to blow, and all traffic came to a halt.

square brackets See **brackets**.

typing More and more people are using typewriter and computer keyboards for writing. Here are a few pointers.

1. Leave at least a 1.5 inch (4 cm) margin on all sides of the
paper. Double-space lines, except in letters, which should be
single-spaced with double-spacing between paragraphs and
headings. Do not type on both sides of the paper.

2. Indent the start of each paragraph five spaces.

3. Two spaces follow the punctuation which marks the end
of a sentence, unless it is followed by a closing quotation mark
(in which case, the two spaces follow the quotation mark). One
space follows punctuation marks within a sentence, e.g. the
comma, the semi-colon, and the colon. No space is needed
after an apostrophe or an opening parenthesis, bracket, or
quotation mark. In the examples below, # marks a space.

He sat down.##She got up;#she paced the floor.##
Must we resort to violence?##Where will it end?##
All three were there:#Mary,#Martha,#and Molly.##
"Well,"#he answered,#"one of us#(I won't say
   who)#is lying."##

4. Many typing keyboards do not have the number 1. Use a lower-case L (l), *not* a capital I. (The latter is reserved for the Roman numeral I.)

5. Never type corrections over mistakes. If looks are unimportant, ex over the offending word or phrase, and retype it correctly immediately afterwards. For a neater appearance, use one of the handy correcting fluids or films to blank out the mistake, then retype on top of this.

Dialects

My childhood was spent in the Eastern Townships of Quebec, an area just north of Vermont that was settled by English-speaking Loyalists after the US War of Independence. We often used to cross the border to drive into Vermont. I was always struck by the distinctive sounds of the New Englanders' speech—undoubtedly related to my Canadian, but clearly different. Here, a scant twenty-five miles from my home, they said "te-MAY-tuh" where we always said "te-MAT-o", "TOOS-dee" instead of "TYOUS-day" and "HAY-end" instead of "hand". The invisible and largely meaningless political border between the two nations was nevertheless a clearly perceptible speech frontier.

The contrast between the English dialects of Quebec and Vermont is nothing compared with that between those of North Wales and South Carolina, Scotland and Nova Scotia, or Texas and Tasmania. English, a language which began as a German-related dialect in south-eastern Britain more than a millennium ago, is today the most widespread and influential language of the world.

Yet, there has never been one pure English, even in written form. Old English (or Anglo-Saxon) grew out of the invading Angles and Saxons' Germanic dialects. Anglo-Saxon monarchs gradually increased their hold over more and more of present-day England, Wales, Scotland, and Ireland, until 1066, when French-speaking Norman invaders took control of the English monarchy. Norman French became the norm at court and among the leaders of the land, but English always remained the language of the people. By the fourteenth century, many different dialects of Middle English had been recorded in manuscripts which are still preserved. The anonymous fourteenth-century poet who wrote the stirring tale of *Sir Gawain and the Green Knight* lived two hundred miles northwest of London, near present-day Liverpool. Without long and arduous study, the Gawain-poet's dialect is virtually incomprehensible to us today. Chaucer, in London, was writing *The Canterbury Tales* at the same time, but Chaucer's Middle English, by comparison, is still fairly easy to read. This is because Chaucer wrote in the dialect of England's ruling class. The dialect of the London court, minor aristocracy, and gentry has since Chaucer's time at least typified a kind of standard British English. Standard English spelling, syntax, and vocabulary became standard only after first having become established in the usage of educated upper-class Londoners.

The greatest concentration of English dialects, by which I mean pronunciation, vocabulary, and idiomatic usage, is still to be found in the "Old Country"—the present-day island nations of Eire and the United Kingdom. Travel fifty miles, and you'll hear the difference—sometimes a great deal of difference. Even a non-specialist ear soon learns to distinguish between major dialects: Educated London, Cockney, West Country, West Midland, East Midland, Northern, Welsh, Scots, and Irish English. At times, the dialect's features, the sounds that make it distinctive, may virtually obscure the underlying English. I recall two experiences. In one, I was standing in the Central Wales market town of Builth listening to a group of local women talking Welsh (my grandmother's native tongue, and one I understand a little)—or so I thought. Only after some moments of this did I realize that they were really talking English. On another occasion, in Aberdeen airport, I found myself in conversation with a farmer and his two sons from somewhere to the north-west, scarcely a word of whose English could I understand, though they seemed to have little trouble understanding me. We spent a convivial hour together, though it was rather tense when I could tell by intonation and facial expression that I had been asked a question.

The first significant movement of English to places beyond

the British Isles was to North America, to the present-day nations of Canada and the United States of America. The English of this wave, which began in the seventeenth century, has evolved over the centuries into a group of dialects we call American English. Today, American English is the speech of a majority of the world's English speakers, though British English remains more widely distributed. The influence of US film, radio, and television productions has made the sounds of the four main American dialects (Northern, Midland, Highland Southern, and Coastal Southern) familiar to English-speakers all over the world. On the other hand, the typical American speaker would have trouble understanding the distinctive British English dialects of such places as Stepney, Stoke-on-Trent, Glasgow, Cardiff, Durban, Wellington, and Wollongong.

The most common divergences between British and American vocabulary are well-enough known. These are a few of them:

American	British
billion	thousand million
trillion	billion (million million)
elevator	lift
first floor	ground floor
second floor	first floor
sidewalk	pavement
pavement	tarmac
yard	garden
garden	flower (or vegetable) garden
laundromat	launderette
suspenders	braces
faucet	tap
gasoline	petrol
kerosene	paraffin
paraffin	paraffin wax
truck	lorry
raincoat	macintosh
two weeks	fortnight

Another divergence lies in distinctive American spellings for certain words. This is mainly the work of Noah Webster, best known for his American English dictionary, first published in 1828, in which the new, streamlined spellings were used. For decades, Webster carried on a one-man campaign to have his "improved" spellings of certain words adopted generally, and some are indeed now standard American spellings. Yet Webster insisted in the Preface to his dictionary, "the body of the language is the same [in America] as in England, and it is desirable to perpetuate that sameness." It is not clear why he felt these spelling variants would contribute to this sameness. Here are some of Webster's changes which have been adopted in the US:

1. Some British spellings ending in *-our* change to American *-or*:

> honour, honor   colour, color   parlour, parlor
> But note: *honorarium* and *honorary* are standard
> everywhere.

2. Some British *-re* endings change to *-er*:

> centre, center   fibre, fiber   metre, meter
> theatre, theater   litre, liter   sombre, somber

3. British may keep while American may drop a final *e* when *-able* is added.

> British: blameable, likeable
> American: blamable, likable

4. American spelling has departed from the standard use of *c* and *s* to distinguish between related nouns and verbs, as shown in these examples:

> advice (noun)   (This example demonstrates the stan-
> advise (verb)   dard rule: a *c* denotes a noun, an *s* a verb.)
>
> defence   (Brit. noun)
> defense   (Amer. noun and verb)

licence	(Brit. noun, Amer. noun and verb)
license	(Brit. verb)
practice	(Brit. noun, Amer. noun and verb)
practise	(Brit. verb)

The truth is, English spelling has never been anything but chaotic, and Webster's American innovations only made a messy situation worse. Fortunately, anyone who can read English can usually accommodate a certain amount of alien spelling or punctuation without too much difficulty—as long as the writer is consistent. The main regret is that it all adds to the gargantuan task of mastering standard English spelling.

Here are some common words with distinctive British/American spellings:

American	British
ax	axe
check (bank)	cheque
disk	disc
jail	gaol (now becoming rare)
jewelry	jewellery
mold	mould
plow	plough
skeptic	sceptic
story (of a building)	storey
tire (car)	tyre
traveler	traveller

British and American placing of **quotation marks** and **hyphens** sometimes also differs: see TYPOGRAPHY under these headings.

British and American also differ in the way certain prepositions are used. For example, American informally adds *of* to phrases such as *all of the men* and *off of the table*, where British, even informally, would be more likely to say *all the men* and *off the table*. On the other hand, American says *out the window* not *out of the window*, as does British. American speaks of protesting war,

British of protesting against it. The potential for international misunderstanding, especially at the highest political levels, is immense.

By far the largest national group of American English speakers is made up of the population of the USA. In fact, US folk outnumber all the rest of the native English-speakers of the world (though the balance is redressed if we include the large number of English-speakers in India, Pakistan, and many African countries where English is used as an internal means of communication between people with differing native tongues). American English is used in only one other large country: Canada. Even there, some British spelling and vocabulary still survive. As opposed to the US's four main dialects and various sub-dialects (such as those of New York City and Maine), Canada has only one dialect, a variant of US Northern, with one easily distinguishable sub-dialect, that of Newfoundland (and, to a lesser degree, the other Atlantic provinces). Although British and American spelling and punctuation are equally acceptable, Canadians may still use British conventions when they write, preferring the British spellings axe, centre, and traveller, to the American ax, center, and traveler, for example. And Canadians, like all British-English speakers the world over, say "zed" for the last letter of the alphabet, as opposed to "zee" in the USA (though this too may be changing as a result of *Sesame Street* and American television generally).

Later waves of British emigration took English to South Africa, Australia, New Zealand, and other parts of what became the British Empire. Written English in these countries, and in others such as India, Hong Kong, Jamaica, Belize, and Bermuda, has generally maintained the conventions of British usage, though each nation has its own spoken English dialect, often quite unintelligible to a visitor. South African English has been influenced by the sound and vocabulary of Afrikaans, a dialect of Dutch which now has the status of a separate language. Australian English shows little regional variation, though upward socio-economic mobility in Australia is often accompanied by use of the pronunciation and vocabulary of Educated London rather than what is termed broad Australian or "Strine". New Zealand English is similar to Australian. (It is about as easy for a British-English speaker to distinguish between Canadian and US dialects as it is for an American-English speaker to distinguish between those of Australia and New Zealand.)

In the 1920s, two scholars, C. K. Ogden and I. A. Richards, proposed a streamlined version of our language, called Basic English, to be used as an international medium of communication. Basic English contains 850 words, including 600 nouns and 150 adjectives. There are only 16 verbs, which relieves the learner of the burden of having to cope with the many irregular verbs in our language. The greater part of this vocabulary, which is said to be suitable for most communications, is familiar to the average English-speaking six-year-old. Beyond this basic vocabulary, there are 100 general science words and 250 idiomatic expressions which must be mastered. Basic English is not a particularly attractive sort of English, nor is it all that easy to use well, but it is certainly a useful language of communication between non-English-speaking nations, or even within a single country such as India where many languages are spoken. English is more immediately useful for this purpose than is an artificial language such as Esperanto. Best of all, students who begin with Basic English already have a good start on eventually mastering the greater language.

Style

Most guides to good writing will tell you to aim for simplicity, directness, and clarity. This boils down to one thing, really: what you write must above all be interesting to a reader. That's all there is to it. How to accomplish this? Here are a few tips that may help.

When you have something to write, the first step is to find a place where you can be left alone for a while. This may not be so simple, particularly if you have young children or work in an overcrowded office, but it's something to aim for. At least you'll learn to develop your powers of concentration if you don't find an ideal spot right away.

Have plenty of paper handy, as well as your dictionary and other relevant reference books, and something to write with. Be sure your body is comfortable and the lighting good. Then just begin. Don't be in the least critical—start with separate words if whole sentences don't come to you. Then build on some of the key words. Don't worry about quality yet—this is just the warm-up. You might get a few brilliant ideas at this point, but don't worry if you don't. Write down everything you can think of that you might want to use—notes or fragments of sentences will do. You can't tell at this stage what may turn out to be useful in the end, so don't try.

As soon as you've done this, without any delay, start writing your first draft. You may already begin to see what your main points really are. Try, as you go, to arrange them in the most effective order. (Of course, you may end up changing them later too.) Whatever your state of mind, concentrate on writing the whole thing out in full, developing it into sentences and paragraphs, and remembering that each paragraph is supposed to mark a clear step forward. Double-space lines to allow plenty of room for changes later. Push yourself on to some kind of ending, whatever happens, and don't stop before then. Don't be over-critical: this is merely the end of stage one. Now put this draft away for a few days, and think of other things.

After a suitable interval, with mind refreshed, return to your chosen workplace with your first draft. Read it over thoroughly and minutely. Here and there you may be able to think of a better word or phrase. Write the changes in. Cross out words and sentences that contribute nothing. Check any word whose spelling seems dubious. Above all, look hard at the order of your main points. Is it effective? Is anything material missing? Is anything irrelevant included? Anything repeated? You may find it useful to cut the first draft up into paragraphs, or even parts of paragraphs, and then to experiment by placing them in different orders to see which seems to work best.

Now take up the emended material, arranged in the most effective order. Begin a second draft, based on this material— but this time try to pull it into something more like a finished piece. Don't close the door on any new ideas you may have even this late, and don't hesitate to throw out anything that does not pull its weight. Throughout all this, try to be aware of the structure of the final piece.

The worst is over. If you have time, put your second draft away, preferably for at least a week. (If you feel driven to work on it sooner, nothing I say will stop you anyway.) Then get it out. READ THE WHOLE THING OUT LOUD. LISTEN CLOSELY TO WHAT IT COMMUNI-CATES. (Even better: ask a friend to read it to you.) Does it say what you meant? Does the reader's voice flounder, sound puzzled, or run out of breath? These may be clues to typographical faults such as omitted words or misspellings, or could indicate that something still needs to be rewritten. Try to approach your work with the eyes and ears of a reader who knows nothing whatever about you or your subject. Be sure the paths of your argument are well marked. Cut out clichés and other lapses of good taste. What tone of voice do you seek to convey? Is it objective, formal, businesslike? Or subjective, informal, friendly? Be consistent in maintaining the tone you feel to be most in harmony with your subject and your reader.

Now, cut this second draft up into paragraphs and rearrange once again if the order still doesn't seem the best. You may experience moments of revelation even this late in the process—suddenly realizing, for example, that a piece of information you put way down towards the end is actually the most interesting part of all and should be moved to the beginning. (A journalist's eye for a "lead" is a great asset here.) Passages that seemed brilliant when you wrote them may have lost some of their sparkle—rewrite them or throw them out. Remember your goals of simplicity, directness, and clarity. Then, when you are ready, use this emended second draft as the basis of your final draft. Write or type it out neatly, following any editorial style guides provided with the assignment.

It's best if you can put the final draft away for a while, too, for at least a few days. Then read it through carefully one last time. This is essential—new mistakes may have crept in. A small number of emendations may be inserted, on separate pages if necessary, so with luck you won't have to rewrite or retype the whole thing. At a certain point you will know that the piece is probably as good as it will ever be—and this is when to stop. Most writing may be "improved" *ad infinitum*, but you have to decide when enough is enough. Now your creation will have to stand alone, whether it be as informal letter (for which one draft is normally enough), history essay, job application, scholarly article, or company report.

All conscientious writers, even the most famous and most highly regarded, write draft after draft. It's simply a fact of life. The writer with the biggest problem is the one who begins with the assumption that you only need to write a thing once to get it right. Effective writing is not easy, as Robert Clairborne points out:

When we are talking face to face, or even phone to phone, misunderstandings can be dealt with and corrected immediately. In writing, if we don't make ourselves clear, there is no easy way – often no way at all – to set matters right. In short, if to speak and to speak well are two things, to write well is yet another thing, whose essential quality was summed up by the Roman orator Cicero some two thousand years ago: the aim of writing is not simply to be understood, but to make it impossible to be *mis*understood.*

When people speak of a writing style they mean something akin to a fingerprint, something in the writing that says, "This writer is a real person." For every individual, the best writing style is the one that seems the least self-conscious, the most natural and unaffected. So concentrate on writing as briefly, simply, and meaningfully as possible, seeking continually to keep your reader interested, and your style will take care of itself.

Some people hanker after writing careers. Writing professionally demands daily exercise, just as does any other complex skill. You have to be willing to take it seriously and attend to it regularly. Don't be discouraged by your first attempts, as long as you give them your best. If you keep at it, your chances of success are excellent. The hardest thing for would-be writers to understand is that while talent helps, the chief prerequisites are really faith in oneself and the will to endure.

* *Our Marvelous Native Tongue,* p. 297.

Writing Letters and Other Pieces

Business letters

Every firm and organization has its own format for correspondence. The style presented below is only one of many, but it has the virtue of being simple and efficient to duplicate.

137 Pickwick Lane
Hamilton, Bermuda
27 January 1987

The Manager
Bender Brakes, Ltd
P.O. Box 9797
Kingston, Jamaica

Dear Manager,

In October 1986 I placed an order with you for ....
....
....

I would be grateful if you would ....
....

Yours sincerely,

Paula White
(Mrs. Gordon White)

Writing Letters and Other Pieces

Note:

1. The entire letter (if typed) is single-spaced, with three line-spaces after the recipient's address, and double spaces between paragraphs and other parts of the letter. Margins should be at least 1.5 inches (4 cm) on all sides, wider if the letter is a short one taking up less than a page. Paragraphs need not be indented. (Alternative: double-space the whole letter, and indent each paragraph five spaces.) Leave enough space after the complimentary close ("Yours sincerely") to allow for signature.

2. Return address is on right. Give in full, including postal code, if any. Your telephone number may also be included after the address and before the date if there is a chance that the recipient may find it more convenient to phone rather than write back to you.

3. Recipient's address follows, on left side. Give in full, just as it will appear on the envelope. If an individual's name is part of the address, use either American or British styles of address:

Mr. John Smith (American)   John Smith, Esq. (British).

Alternatively, and increasingly nowadays, honorifics such as Mr. and Esq. are being omitted altogether, though older people may still find this over-casual.

4. The appropriate salutation is Dear, followed by the name of the individual or position, as the examples below show:

Dear Mr. Smith (both American and British)
Dear Mrs. White
Dear Ms. Flanagan
Dear Manager (if the position, but not the name, is
    known)
Dear Flowell Valves (if only the name of the firm is
    known).

Note: It is *always* more effective if your letter can be directed to an individual person by name. (You may have to do some research, possibly by phone, to find out the correctly spelled name of the individual you should be addressing.) Letters addressed merely to a position or to a firm tend to go unread.

5. Keep the body of the letter as short and simple as possible. General advice for writing is given in STYLE, starting on page 155. A common plan for a business letter is:

First paragraph: acknowledge whatever communication immediately preceded this letter, quoting date and any reference number. This enables the recipient to link your letter to what has gone before.

Second and subsequent paragraphs: state your reason for writing now. Make sure this is perfectly clear. Don't worry about "dressing up" your language. The simplest words are still usually the best.

Final paragraph: briefly close with some suggestion of what you are expecting to follow. For example, "I look forward to hearing from you as soon as you are able to arrive at an estimate for this job," or, "I apologize for this confusion, and hope to see you next week."

6. The standard complimentary close for both business and social letters is "Yours sincerely," though there are many others. ("Yours faithfully," is widely used in the UK.) Be guided by other correspondence you have received, particularly anything written by the party you are now addressing.

7. Your name need not be typed after the signature, as long as your signature is quite legible. You may, if you have one, wish to type the title of your position, e.g. Manager, President, Professor. Women should spell out the form of their name they wish to be addressed by, putting the honorific in parentheses. Men need not bother with the honorific, unless it is something other than "Mr."

> (Miss) Penny Cartwright
> (Ms.) Rachael Berney Roberts
> (Mrs.) Ersall Twing
> (Mrs.) Minnie Twing (widow or divorcee)
> (Dr.) U. B. Well

Writing Letters and Other Pieces

Personal letters

The layout for personal letters is simpler than that for business letters. The return address is set on the right, just as in business letters, with the date following. (If you are writing to a regular correspondent and your address has not changed, the date alone will usually suffice.) The recipient's address is not normally part of a personal address; instead you should proceed directly to the salutation:

> Dear Miss Jones,
> Dear Penny,
> Dear Dad,

followed by the body of the letter, arranged in paragraphs. An informal personal letter is usually pretty much of a spontaneous creation, and a certain amount of crossing-out and other emendation is quite acceptable, as long as the end result remains legible. If you are writing to a relative stranger, however, or if you are writing about something important, it may be as well to make a clean copy of the final version. Many important personal letters are written in haste, and their writers might consider putting them away at least overnight in order to consider whether the best approach has been taken.

Whatever else is required of a personal letter, it should be interesting to its reader. There is no point at all in sending a boring or ill-considered letter.

Your letter may conclude with "Yours sincerely," or any other one of the many personal complimentary closes. It is rarely necessary to type or print your name beneath your signature, unless you are writing to a relative stranger.

Envelopes

The standard international form for either a business or a personal letter is:

Michael Nichols
123 Any Street
Anytown, Anywhere

Mrs. Joan Borridge
197 Honeysuckle St
Dublin, Eire

Note that correspondents in Australia, Eire, New Zealand and the UK usually write or type their return address on the back of the envelope rather than the front:

Michael Nichols, 123 Any Street, Anytown, Anywhere

Michael Nichols
123 Any Street
Anytown
Anywhere

It goes without saying that all envelopes should bear a return address, in case the letter does not reach the addressee for some reason. Postal code, if any, should be included.

Other pieces

Under this heading I include company reports, high-school compositions, university essays, graduate research pieces, scientific articles, and all forms of literature. Whatever their form, universal principles of expression apply. See more on this under STYLE, page 155–8. The following section is concerned only with some of the more mechanical aspects of presentation.

1. Title page

Type the title of your piece about one-third of the way down your title page, capitalizing important words. (Do not underline: this is reserved for works that have already been published.) Your name goes two-thirds of the way down. Further information (your address and phone number, the name of the course for which the piece is required, the name of your agent, etc.) may go in a single-spaced block at the bottom right of the page.

2. Body

Begin the main part of your piece on page 2 (page 1 is the title). Double-space, and indent paragraphs five spaces. Leave at least 1.5 inches (4 cm) margin on all sides.

3. Quotations

These should be exact. See TYPOGRAPHY under **quotation marks**, for more on the conventions of quotation; also see FURTHER READING for the main general reference works you are likely to encounter. If you are quoting more than two lines of poetry or ten lines of prose, set the quoted material in an indented block, single-spaced, without using quotation marks. Otherwise, use quotation marks and incorporate the quoted material into your text. (The mark / is used to indicate the ends of lines of poetry when it is quoted as part of the text; e.g. "Thirty days hath September,/ April, June, and November.") References to footnotes, made as superscript numbers, should immediately follow the end of the quotation or relevant section of your piece, like this:[1].

4. Footnotes

These (if any) may go either at the bottom of the page where they are cited, or in a group at the end of the whole piece.

(The latter is easier if you are typing, but is more demanding of your reader.) Number footnotes consecutively through a whole piece, if it is short, or through a whole chapter or section of a longer work. Here are some standard footnotes:

1. Jessie Benson, *Life in the Mato Grosso* (New York, 1978), p. 75.
2. E. A. Sprigg, "New Pagodas," *Journal of Architecture* 23 (June 1982), 97–8.
3. *The Oxford English Dictionary*, "footnotes".

Written or typed titles of published volumes, including magazines and other periodicals, are underlined, denoting italics. Articles and shorter pieces occurring within a volume are in quotation marks. The second example shows this: note that the number which follows the title of a journal is the volume number, and the second number is the page reference (the abbreviation p. is not needed in citations of periodicals). The third example gives, rather than a page number, a reference to an entry, "footnotes". For further information, see FURTHER READING.

5. Bibliography

This follows the body of the piece, and is normally limited to works which you have already cited in footnotes. The layout of a bibliography entry is quite similar to that of a footnote, except the author's surname is placed first, and the whole list is arranged alphabetically. No book page references are given. In the case of an article, the page extent of the whole article should be given.

Benson, Jessie, *Life in the Mato Grosso* (New York, 1978).
Oxford English Dictionary, The.
Sprigg, E. A., "New Pagodas," *Journal of Architecture* 23 (June 1982), 92–107.

For further information, see FURTHER READING.

6. Abbreviations

In general, you should confine yourself to abbreviations which are commonly understood. Latinate scholarly abbreviations such as op. cit. and ibid. have now fallen from grace (and others such as e.g., i.e., viz., et al., and even etc. may eventually follow them into oblivion). Any reference, whether in a footnote or in the text, to an article or book already mentioned requires no more than a short title of your own devising: (Benson, p. 79) or ("New Pagodas," 102), for example.

Your aim throughout should be to make things as clear as possible for your reader. Aimless footnotes and references which interrupt the reader's perusal of your main text should be avoided if at all possible, especially if their main function is simply to impress the writer's supposed erudition on a marvelling world.

7. *Copies*

If the letter or article you are writing is important, you will certainly want to keep a copy of it, either by making a carbon copy of your final version, or by photocopying the original.

Note that many businesses, particularly publishing firms, will not acknowledge unsolicited articles or other pieces of writing (including, sometimes, even letters) unless they have been accompanied by a stamped self-addressed envelope from the sender. If you are sending an unsolicited manuscript for consideration, you must include a self-addressed stamped envelope, with sufficient postage for the weight of the manuscript. International Reply Coupons, available at any post office, must be included if you are sending your manuscript to another country. It will almost certainly vanish without trace otherwise.

For tips on typing (including computer keyboarding) of text, see TYPOGRAPHY, under **typing**.

Glossary of Grammatical Terms

abstract noun   See **noun**.

active voice   Sentences with **transitive verb predicates** (those that require an object) are usually expressed in such a way that the subject acts upon the object. *Higgins* [subject] *painted* [predicate] *the room* [object]. This is the active voice, and is usually the more direct and lively way to express this grammatical relationship. See also **passive voice**.

adjective   is a word (or group of words) modifying the meaning of a noun: *He is a happy* (adjective) *man* (noun). *Happy* is the **positive form** of a **descriptive adjective**, simply describing the noun it modifies. Descriptive adjectives may also be **comparative** or **superlative** in **degree**: *the happier* [comparative] *of the two children, the happiest* [superlative] *man in the world*. The alternative forms *more happy, (the) most happy* may also be used to compare adverbs: *more happily, most happily*. See also **possessive adjective**.

adjective phrase   See **phrase** for the modern sense, **preposition** for the traditional one.

adverb   is a word (or group of words) that qualifies or modifies the meaning of a verb or adjective. Many, but by no means all, adverbs end in *-ly: He knocked loudly* [adverb]. *His somewhat* [adverb] *unpleasant* [adjective] *manner upset me*.

adverb phrase   See **phrase** for the modern sense, **preposition** for the traditional one.

article   in English may be either **definite** *(the), or* **indefinite** *(a, an).* The article is one of the class of limiting adjectives.

auxiliary verb   is a type of **grammatical verb** that modifies the effect of a **lexical verb** with which it is used. In English, the most common auxiliary verbs are *be, have,* and *do* (the latter usually limited to emphatic, interrogative, and negative forms): I *am* coming, she *has* been, I *do* care, I *don't* worry, *do* they want any?

clause   A clause is a group of words that includes a subject and a predicate. A sentence may contain one or more clauses, but at least one of these must be **independent;** that is, capable of standing on its own as a meaningful and complete sentence. Clauses introduced by **subordinating conjunctions** such as *if* or *whenever* are called **dependent;** their meaning depends on the presence of an independent clause in the same sentence: *They will go* [independent clause] *if they are asked* [dependent clause].

colloquial   refers to informal or conversational usage. For example, contractions such as *don't* and *they're* are colloquial and not acceptable in formal writing. Colloquialisms are fine in an informal context.

common noun   See **noun.**

comparative   See **adjective.**

complement   The complement of the subject of a sentence is the adjective (or group of words functioning as an adjective) that follows a linking **verb.** In the sentences *Mary is pale* and *I am becoming sick and tired of this nonsense, pale* and *becoming sick and tired of this nonsense* are complements, qualifying the subjects *Mary* and *I.*

concrete noun   See **noun.**

conditional   is a form of the finite verb suggesting dependence on some other hypothetical verb (which itself may be expressed in **subjunctive mood** or in the **past perfect tense**): *he would go* [conditional] *if he were able* [subjunctive]; *he would have gone* [conditional past] *if he had been able* [past perfect].

conjunction   A **co-ordinating conjunction** joins two things of the same grammatical rank: Tom *and* Jerry, coming *or* going, over the river *and* through the woods. Some co-ordinating conjunctions, called **correlatives**, are used in pairs: *either* come *or* go; *both* he *and* I went. A **subordinating conjunction** joins two **clauses** of a sentence in such a way as to show some kind of inequality or dependence in the relationship: I see him [clause] *whenever* I get the chance [clause]. The subordinating conjunction *whenever* in the last example shows the second clause is dependent on the first.

conjunctive adverb   is a type of **subordinating conjunction**, an adverb that joins two clauses of a sentence. Common examples are *however, moreover*, and *nevertheless*. A conjunctive adverb is usually preceded by a semi-colon and followed by a comma: *I have had nothing to eat; moreover, I am tired. I will tolerate no more excuses; however, I agree to hearing your explanation.*

declarative   Sentences that are declarative state something: *It's going to rain. She has written three novels.* The usual order of a simple declarative sentence in English is Subject + Predicate + Object or Complement (if present).

definite article   See **article**.

degree   See **adjective**.

demonstrative adjectives and pronouns contrast two objects, a nearer and a farther. They are *this* and *that* (singular) and

dependent clause

these and *those* (plural): *Give me that* [adjective] *record. Pass me those* [pronoun].

dependent clause   See **clause**.

dialect   The actual form of a language spoken by people of a particular geographical or socio-economic group, for example, Cockney, Irish, Australian, New England, Canadian. The language of the best-educated in any country, though no less a dialect itself, gives rise to an abstraction we call the standard form of that language. In this book, English is divided into two super-dialects, American and British, with those elements that are common to both making up what we call standard English. Standard English is the language of communication between people of different English dialects, and, increasingly, between non-English-speaking nations having no other common language.

ellipsis   A group of three points indicating that something has been omitted from a sentence. See TYPOGRAPHY under **point**.

emphatic   The form of the verb used when extra emphasis is required: *he does paint* [present emphatic], *he did paint* [past emphatic].

future, future perfect   See **tense**.

gerund   The noun form of a **lexical verb**, a gerund always ends in *-ing*. So does the **present participle** form, but the functions of the two are different. In *Running is his hobby* the word *running* is a gerund, but in *I saw him running* it is a present participle.

grammar   A codification of principles observed in the way people speak and write any given language. "It is not the business of grammar, as some critics seem preposterously to imagine, to give law to the fashions which regulate our speech. On the contrary, from its conformity to these, and from that alone, grammar derives all its authority and value."—George Campbell, *The Philosophy of Rhetoric*.

grammatical verb   A general term covering both **auxiliary verbs** and **linking verbs**, in contrast to **lexical verbs**. See under each of these terms for further information.

imperfect   A form of past tense showing that action was in progress when something else happened: *he was painting (when I saw him)*. See also **progressive**.

indefinite adjectives and pronouns   refer to singular or plural entities in general, rather than specifically. Examples are *each, many, none, few, all, some*, and *any. Many* [adjective] *people called. Many* [pronoun] *called.*

indefinite article   See **article**.

independent clause   See **clause**.

indicative   See **mood**.

infinitive   is the "raw" form of a verb, referring to no particular subject or time; often, but not always, preceded by *to*: *to love, to go, to have, to be*. The infinitive may be used as a noun: *To err* [infinitive] *is human*. It is also commonly used as part of a combination following a finite verb: *I am going* [present continuous] *to tell* [infinitive] *him*. In this example the combination *am going to tell* is the predicate of the sentence, *I* the subject, and *him* the object.

interjection   is a word or group of words used as some kind of emotional outburst: *Whew! Wow! Yum yum!*

interrogative adverbs   ask something about the predicate of a sentence: *How* did she do it? *Why* are you crying? *When* will he ever go?

interrogative pronouns   ask questions about the object of the the predicate: *Who* has the map? *What* are you doing? *Which* do you want?

interrogative sentence   An interrogative sentence is one that asks something: *Have we any eggs? Can Barry clean the fish?* In such a sentence, an auxiliary verb usually precedes the subject, as in the second example where the auxiliary *can* precedes the subject *Barry* and the infinitive *clean* follows it. If no auxiliary verb occurs in the declarative form of the sentence, the interrogative form typically inserts a form of *do* to serve as auxiliary: Declarative: *He* [subject] *runs* [lexical verb] *to work.* Interrogative: *Does* [auxiliary] *he* [subject] *run* [lexical verb] *to work?* The only exception to this rule is when a lexical verb itself is also a common auxiliary (*be, have*): *Is he tired? Has he the money?* Even so, in the case of *have*, the auxiliary *do* is often added: *Does* [auxiliary] *he* [subject] *have* [lexical verb] *the money?* OR *Has* [auxiliary] *he* [subject] *got* [lexical verb] *the money?*

intransitive verbs   are lexical verbs that do not require an object: *John wept, the cat yawned.*

irregular verbs   are verbs whose past and past participle forms are formed in some way other than by adding *-(e)d* to the infinitive. A list of the main irregular verbs in English is given on the inside back cover. See also **principal parts**.

lexical verbs   are those which communicate individual specific meanings; they are contrasted with **auxiliary verbs** and **linking verbs**, whose function in a sentence is to modify the other words of the sentence in some way. In the sentence *Mr Briggs was furious when he saw John had stolen the apples*, the lexical verb is *stolen* (the past participle of *steal*). The other verbs in the sentence are linking (*was*) and auxiliary (*had*). Lexical verbs have meaning even in isolation, the sort of independent meaning we may look up in a dictionary. They are also known as **principal verbs**.

limiting adjective   See **article** and **possessive adjective**.

linking verb   is usually a form of the verb *to be*, though other verbs such as *appear*, *look*, and *seem* are also common linking verbs. In such sentences as *You are tired*, *She appeared angry*, *He looks sick* and *They seem happy*, these verbs link their subjects to some kind of descriptive adjective, termed the **complement** of the subject. Symbolically, the linking verb may be thought of as something of an equal sign: *You = tired*, *She = angry*, *He = sick*, *They = happy*. Traditionally, this form was known as the copula, or copulative verb, from the Latin, *copulare*, to couple or join together.

modifier   A word (or group of words) preceding another word and in some way affecting its meaning. In *the most untidy child* the first three words (an adjective phrase) modify the last. Opposed to **qualifier**, which follows the word it affects.

mood   The mood of a verb expresses the attitude of the speaker towards what the verb expresses. The moods in English are **indicative** (having to do with fact), **subjunctive** (having to do with desire, hypothesis, or supposition), and **imperative** (conveying an order). In Latin and many present-day European languages, mood is shown by different verb endings; in English, however, it is usually conveyed (if by other than context alone) by the use of auxiliary verbs such as *may*, *might*, and *should*. In particular, the subjunctive form is rarely distinguished from that of the indicative except in the 1st and 3rd person singular forms of the verb *to be*: *Henry was king*, *I was to come by three* (indicative); *if Henry were king*, *if he were to come by three* (subjunctive). The imperative is formed by dropping *-(e)s* from the 3rd person singular indicative: *He hits the ball* [indicative]. *Hit the ball!* [imperative].

negative In a negative sentence *not* is inserted within the predicate, usually between the auxiliary and the lexical verb. If no auxiliary occurs in the declarative form, the auxiliary *do* is used in the negative: *He exercises* [predicate] *enough. He does* [auxiliary] *not* [negative] *exercise* [infinitive] *enough.* If the predicate is itself a common auxiliary (*have, be*) the auxiliary *do* may, strictly speaking, not be needed: *He is old; he is not old. He has enough, he hasn't enough.* Even so, if the verb is *have*, an auxiliary *do* is commonly used in the negative: *He doesn't have enough*; or, alternatively, *he hasn't got enough.*

nominative absolute is a term, derived from Latin grammar, applied to a participial phrase that has no stated grammatical relationship to the rest of the sentence, as in the first five words of the following example: *The train having already left, we had to take a taxi.* In fact, the nominative absolute functions as an adverbial phrase, in this case modifying *had to take.* Use of the nominative absolute in everyday English is rare.

noun is the name of a person or thing. A **proper noun** begins with a capital letter (*Mississippi*); a **common noun** does not (*potato*). A **concrete noun** names something that has material existence (*rock*); an **abstract noun** names something that does not (*trouble*). A regular noun referring to a countable entity is made plural by the addition of *-(e)s* to its singular form.

noun phrase See **phrase** for the modern sense, **preposition** for the traditional one.

number See **person**.

object is the noun (or other word or words doing duty for a noun) acted upon by the main verb (predicate) of a sentence:

He [subject] *is painting* [predicate] *the upstairs bathroom* [object].

object of a preposition   See **preposition**.

parenthesis   A parenthetical expression is a phrase, clause, or sentence included within a sentence that is complete without it: My father, *who had been looking for his glasses*, hit his head. Commas, dashes, or round brackets are commonly used to separate these from the rest of the sentence. (For more on these see the TYPOGRAPHY section.)

participle   A non-finite verb form. In English there are two sorts of participle, **present** (for example, *loving, going, having, being*) and **past** (*loved, gone, had, been*). Present participle forms always end in *-ing*. Most past participles end in *-ed*, but a significant number are irregularly formed, as in the last three of the examples above. See the inside back cover for a more complete list.

passive voice   Sentences with transitive verbs (those followed by an object) are usually expressed in an active form: *We* [subject] *prepared* [predicate] *the contract* [object], with the subject acting upon the object. Any active sentence may, however, also be expressed passively so that the subject is acted upon by the object of the sentence: *The contract* [subject] *was prepared* [predicate] *by us* [object]. The impact of the passive is more diffuse than that of the active, and it is a detriment to lively and interesting writing. At times, however, its use may be unavoidable.

past, past perfect   See **tense**.

perfect   See **tense**.

person   Pronouns in English are classified by person and number. The 1st person pronouns are *I*, *me*, *my* (singular) and *we*, *us*, *our* (plural). (These are, respectively, subject, object, and possessive forms.) The 2nd person singular and plural forms are identical: *you*, *you*, *your*. The 3rd person singular pronouns are *he*, *him*, *his*; *she*, *her*, *her*; and *it*, *it*, *its*; while 3rd person plural pronouns are *they*, *them*, *their*. In many languages verb endings change according to person and number; in English, however, the only usual significant change is in the 3rd person singular present indicative form, which adds -*(e)s* to the infinitive.

phrase   traditionally refers to a group of words that begins with a **preposition**, is followed by a noun, and functions as an adjective, adverb, or noun. (See more under **preposition**.) Modern grammar, however, uses the term more loosely to mean any group of words functioning as a single grammatical entity. For example, in the sentence *Trying your best but refusing to do better is not good enough*, the first eight words form a noun phrase functioning as a single noun that could be replaced by a single pronoun: *It is not good enough*.

possessive adjective   is related in form to the **possessive pronoun**, but precedes and thereby modifies a noun: *It is my* [possessive adjective] *book*. A possessive pronoun, on the other hand, stands alone, doing duty for the possessing noun: *The book is mine* [possessive pronoun].

possessive pronoun   A form of **personal pronoun**, standing for some type of possessing noun, they are: *mine*, *yours*, *his*, *hers*, *its*, *ours*, and *theirs*. See also **possessive adjective** and **pronoun**.

predicate   is the main verb of a sentence. Without a predicate there can be no sentence; even an explicit subject, though present in the majority of English sentences, may be lacking: *Run* [predicate] *to the corner for me*. A sentence may contain more than one predicate: *Mary copied* [predicate] *the letter, mailed* [predicate] *it, and then came* [predicate] *home and made* [predicate] *dinner.* A predicate must be finite: infinitives and participles may not be used as predicates: "Mary copying [present participle] the letter" and "John to have welcomed [past infinitive] James" are not sentences.

preposition shows the relationship between a noun and other nouns in a sentence. Most prepositions have to do with a relationship of space or time: *in, to, under, over, behind, in front of, before,* and *after* are common examples. The **object of a preposition** is the noun or pronoun which follows that preposition, and whole group Preposition + Noun is called a **phrase**. Phrases may function as adjectives (The creature *under the stairs* must be a squirrel), adverbs (I crawled *under the stairs*), or nouns (*Under the stairs* is not a particularly clean spot).

present, present perfect See **tense**.

principal parts of a verb are three: the **infinitive**, the **past**, and the **past participle**. The past and the past participle of a **regular verb** are made by adding *-(e)d* to the infinitive: *move, moved, moved; paint, painted, painted.* Those of an **irregular verb** have to be learned: *lie, lay, lain* and *hit, hit, hit* are examples. (A more complete list of irregular verbs is on the inside back cover of this book.) All tenses of any verb are formed from these three principal parts.

principal verbs See **lexical verbs**.

progressive The form of a verb which shows continuing action: *he is painting* [present progressive], *he was painting* [past progressive, or imperfect], *he will be painting* [future progressive].

pronoun does duty for a noun which has preceded it or

which is at least clearly understood. It has no specific meaning outside of the context in which it occurs. In *Dick hit him,* the pronoun *him* may be understood as referring to someone else. In *I am angry with you, I* is the speaker of the sentence. With the exception of *it,* **personal pronouns** have both subject and object forms: *I, you, he, she, it, we, they* (subject); *me, you, him, her, it, us, them* (object).

proper noun   See **noun**.

qualifier   A word (or group of words) affecting the meaning of a preceding word: the food *I have been eating*, he mused *dreamily*. See also **modifier**.

regular verbs   form their past tense and past participle forms by adding *-(e)d* to the infinitive form: *love* (infinitive), *loved* (past), *loved* (past participle). See also **principal parts**.

relative pronouns   either replace nouns or show the relation between groups of words in a sentence. The main relative pronouns are *who* (used only of persons), *what* (used only of things), and *which* and *that* (used of either persons or things). See VOCABULARY under **that, what, which, who**.

style   In reference to language the term has two separate meanings. The larger, and more common, refers to the distinctive way in which (usually literary) language is used by an individual or a historic group: Dickens's style, the Romantic style. The second has to do with the often arbitrary mechanical conventions of spelling, punctuation, and format used by a specific publisher, journal, or individual: the *Times* style, for example.

subject   is the noun (or words acting as a noun) in a sentence about which the main verb (called the **predicate**) says something. In a conventional declarative sentence, the subject precedes the predicate. An **object** (another noun) will also be required if the predicate is **transitive**: *John* [subject] *sneezed* [predicate]. *Mary* [subject] *caught* [predicate] *the ball* [object].

super-dialect   See **dialect**.

superlative   See **adjective**.

syntax   The convention whereby the order of words or groups of words in a sentence conveys the relationship of their separate meanings to one another. The standard syntax of a simple declarative sentence in English is Subject, Predicate, and (where present) Object or Complement.

tense   The tense of a verb shows its time of action or state of being. The main tenses of the **indicative mood** are **present** (*he paints, he is painting, he does paint*), **past** (*he painted, he did paint*), **future** (*he will paint*), **present perfect** (*he has painted*), **past perfect** (*he had painted*), and **future perfect** (*he will have painted*). The **conditional** and **conditional past** forms (*he would paint, he would have painted*) are often used in conjunction with **subjunctive mood**.

transitive verbs   act on an object: *Priscilla cooked* [verb] *the ratatouille* [object]. *Most people enjoy* [verb] *eating* [object]. Sentences with transitive verbs may also be expressed in passive form: *The ratatouille was cooked by Priscilla. Eating is enjoyed by most people.*

verb   expresses action or state of being. In English, every sentence must have a **finite verb**, even if it has nothing else: *Go!* Finite verbs are classified as to their **person**, **number**, **tense** and **mood**, and are either **transitive** (those that require an **object**, and that may be expressed either in **active** or **passive** form) or **intransitive** (those that do not). Non-finite verb forms are the infinitive and the participle. For further

voice

information see the separate entries above, or see the index for the relevant pages of the GRAMMAR section of this book.

voice   See **active voice** and **passive voice**.

Further Reading

Dictionaries

The Oxford English Dictionary. The revered parent of all modern English dictionaries. Available at most reference libraries, or in a two-volume microtype edition. Computer database edition now in preparation.

For everyday use:

The American Heritage Dictionary.
The Concise Oxford Dictionary (British).
The Penguin English Dictionary (British).
Webster's New Collegiate Dictionary (Merriam-Webster) (American).
Webster's New 20th Century Dictionary (Collins).

Specialist Dictionaries

Bryson, Bill, *The Penguin Dictionary of Troublesome Words* (Harmondsworth, Penguin, 1984).

Lewis, Norman, *Dictionary of Correct Spelling* (New York, Harper & Row, 1962).

Newmark, Maxim, *Dictionary of Foreign Words and Phrases* (New York, Greenwood, 1957).

Onions, C. T., *The Oxford Dictionary of English Etymology* (Oxford University Press, 1966).

Roget's Thesaurus of Words and Phrases (many publishers). Lists synonyms.

History of English

Barnett, Lincoln, *The Treasury of Our Tongue* (New York, New American Library, 1967).

Further Reading

Baugh, Albert C., *A History of the English Language* (New York, Appleton-Century-Crofts, 2nd edition, 1957). A standard American overview.

Bolton, W. F., ed., *The English Language*, Vol. I (Cambridge, Cambridge University Press, 1966), with D. Crystal, Vol. II (1969).

Clairborne, Robert, *Our Marvelous Native Tongue: The Life and Times of the English Language* (New York, Times Books, 1983). Very readable account of the development of our language.

Moore, John, *You English Words* (New York, Dell, 1965).

Linguistics

Hall, Robert A., Jr., *Linguistics and Your Language* (New York, Doubleday, 1960).

Schlauch, Margaret, *The Gift of Tongues* (New York, Viking, n.d.).

American English

Dillard, J. L., *All-American English* (New York, Random House, 1975).

Mencken, H. F., *The American Language* (1936) and two supplements (1945, 1948); paperback edition (New York, Knopf, 1977).

Moss, Norman, *British/American Dictionary* (London, Hutchinson, 1984).

Williamson, Juanita V., and Burke, Virginia M., eds., *A Various Language* (New York, Holt, Rinehart & Winston, 1971).

Australian English

Johnstone, Grahame, *Australian–English Pocket Oxford Dictionary* (Oxford University Press, 1984).

Wilkes, G. A., *Dictionary of Australian Colloquialisms* (London, Routledge & Kegan Paul, 1978).

Canadian English

Avis, W. S., *et al.*, *Dictionary of Canadianisms on Historical Principles* (Toronto, Macmillan, 1975).

Storey, G. M., *et al.*, *Dictionary of Newfoundland English* (University of Toronto Press, 1982).

Slang

Partridge, Eric, *Dictionary of Slang and Unconventional English*, 8th edition, revised by P. Beale (London, Routledge & Kegan Paul, 1984).

Partridge, Eric, *Slang Today and Yesterday*, 4th ed. (London, Routledge & Kegan Paul, 1970).

Usage

The Associated Press Stylebook (Reading, Mass., Addison-Wesley, 1982).

Bernstein, Theodore M., *The Careful Writer: A Modern Guide to English Usage* (New York, Athenaeum, 1965).

Carey, G. V., *Mind the Stop* (Harmondsworth, Penguin, 1971). An exhaustive guide to British punctuation.

The Chicago Manual of Style (University of Chicago, 1982 or most recent edition). American scholarly writing conventions.

Crystal, David, *Who Cares About English Usage?* (Harmondsworth, Penguin, 1984). A discussion of the major shibboleths in English.

Evans, Bergen, and Evans, Cornelia, *A Dictionary of Contemporary American Usage* (New York, Random House, 1957).

Fernald, James C., *English Grammar Simplified* (revised by Cedric Gale, New York, Funk & Wagnalls, 1963).

Follett, Wilson, *Modern American Usage* (New York, Hill & Wang, 1966).

Gowers, Ernest, *Fowler's Modern English Usage*, 2nd ed. (Oxford University Press, 1965).

Gowers, Ernest, *The Complete Plain Words*, 2nd ed. (Harmondsworth, Penguin Books, 1980).

Howard, Philip, *New Words for Old* (Oxford University Press, 1977).

Jordan, Lewis, ed., *The New York Times Manual of Style and Usage* (New York, Times Books, 1976).

Morris, William, and Morris, Mary, *The Harper Dictionary of American Usage* (New York, Harper & Row, 1975). Highly prescriptive.

Partridge, Eric, *Usage and Abusage* (Harmondsworth, Penguin, 1981).

Potter, Simeon, *Our Language* (Harmondsworth, Penguin, 1950; reissued 1981). A British writer's point of view; somewhat dated.

Safire, William, *On Language* (New York, Avon, 1980).

Strunk, William, and White, E. B., *The Elements of Style*, 3rd ed. (New York, Macmillan, 1979).

The Toronto Star Style Book, ed. Lew Gloin (latest edition).

Further Reading

Weiner, E. S. C., *The Oxford Guide to English Usage* (Oxford University Press, 1983).

Wood, Frederick T., *Current English Usage*, 2nd ed. (London, Papermac, 1981).

Quotations and literary reference

Bartlett's Familiar Quotations (New York, Little, revised edition 1980).

Benet, William R., *Reader's Encyclopedia* (New York, Crowell, 2nd edition, 1965).

The Book Review Digest (New York, Wilson). Arranged by year from 1905.

Brewer's Dictionary of Phrase and Fable (London, Cassell, revised edition 1982).

Contemporary Authors (New York, Gale, latest edition).

Contemporary Poets (London, Macmillan, and New York, St Martin, latest edition).

Drabble, Margaret, ed., *The Oxford Companion to English Literature* (Oxford University Press, 1985).

Gayley, Charles M., *Classic Myths in English Literature* (New York, Longwood, 1977; reproduction of 1911 edition).

Herzberg, M. J., *Reader's Encyclopedia of American Literature* (New York, Crowell, 1962).

Magill, Frank N., *Magill's Quotations in Context* (Portland, Ore., Salem Press, n.d.).

Magill, Frank N., *Masterplots*, 12 volumes (Portland, Ore., Salem Press, revised edition 1976). Plot summaries of over 2,000 literary works.

Mencken, H. L., *A New Dictionary of Quotations* (New York, Knopf, 1942).

The Oxford Dictionary of Quotations (Oxford University Press, revised edition 1979).

The Readers' Guide to Periodical Literature (New York, Wilson). Arranged by year from 1900.

Seldes, George, *The Great Quotations* (Secaucus, N. J., Citadel, 1983).

Shipley, Joseph T., ed., *Dictionary of World Literary Terms* (Boston, Writer, n.d.)

Stevenson, Burton, *Home Book of Quotations, Classical and Modern* (New York, Dodd, revised edition 1984).

Miscellaneous reference (use most recent edition available)

The Encyclopedia Americana.

Encyclopaedia Britannica.

The Canadian Encyclopedia (Edmonton, Hurtig, 1985).

Facts on File. "Dictionaries" on various subjects from archaeology to twentieth-century history, as well as annual yearbooks and News Reference Service.

The Guinness Book of World Records (London, Guinness, and New York, Bantam). Annual editions.

Information Please Almanac (New York, Simon & Schuster, 1979).

Kane, Joseph N., *Famous First Facts* (New York, Wilson, 4th edition 1981).

The News Dictionary. People, places, and events of the previous year.

New Standard Encyclopedia.

Wallechinsky, David, and Irving Wallace, *The Book of Lists* (New York, Morrow, 1977, and later supplements).

Who Was Who (New York, St Martin). Arranged by year.

Who's Who. Various national editions published annually.

Who's Who in the World (New York, Marquis). Published annually.

The World Almanac (New York, World Almanac Publications).

The World Book Encyclopedia.

Most reference libraries will have some of these available. Ask if you can't find what you're looking for. A browse in the reference area may turn up other helpful books. What your library doesn't have may be able to be borrowed for you on an inter-library loan.

Index

Index

Index